D1258672

Stranded In Chicken
A Year On The Road
In
South and North America

By David Rice

SST Publications

Tucson, AZ

Stranded In Chicken
A Year On The Road In South and North America

Copyright © 2014 , David Rice
SST Publications

Text © SST Publications 2014
©2014 David Rice/SST Publications

Book Design
David Hilbert

Published By S S T Publications
8987 E Tanque Verde # 309-377
Tucson, AZ 85749

ISBN # 978-0-9816713-1-4
0-9816713-1-4

Printed in the United States of America

Stranded In Chicken
A Year On The Road
In
South and North America

By David Rice

Part I
Confessions Of A Traveler

But the real travelers are those
only who leave In order to leave;
light hearts, similar to balloons,
they are never separated
from their fate,
and, without knowing why, always
say,
"Let us go on."

From The Voyage,
Les Fleurs du Mal, 1857
Charles Baudelaire

IV

Stranded In Chicken
David Rice

Photos by David Rice

"For my part, I travel not to go anywhere,
but to go.
I travel for travel's sake;
the great affair is to move."

Robert Louis Stevenson
Travels with a Donkey, 1879

The trip of a thousand miles begins with a single step. *Lao Tsu*

1. Planting

I live in the Ozarks of Missouri where I take care of a 100 year-old house in the countryside. I tend a garden while caring for the old farm and I take a rent from my house in the city.

I have always loved the hills of Springfield in late winter and, although I live comfortably in the rural house for most of the year, at times I get restless and feel the need to travel.

Since this account is a confession of sorts, to tell you the truth, travel is more obsession with me than need. You Pisceans and Sagittarians will, I hope, empathize with one born under the sign of the compass rose. I have been around the world more than once and would love to do it again, this time staying completely on the ground.

My tale is one of the traveler. While I neither boast nor apologize, this is my story and for

1

convenience rather than contrition, I will call it the confessions of a traveler.

Garden

The warm winds across the prairie in March usually start the feeling. I will be out planting a vegetable garden and the sun's warm breath comes on the back of my neck like the soft caress of a kitten. I know, however, that before June ends, this kitten will become a tiger that will claw up the dust in my dooryard and scorch the grass and garden beyond my toleration. By July, blistering heat will smother the hills and I will long to be somewhere else. My thoughts will be all about air conditioning and unfortunately my old house has none.

A hot afternoon in April had me sitting on the porch wondering where I was going to go next. I have made many long trips throughout the world and I know that to make an extended trip I would need to arrange many details. Africa kept coming to mind as I read the guidebooks. I started to make plans for a trip to the southern parts of Africa.

Details

First I arranged to visit my doctor and get the needed shots. Rabies topped the list because of the wild dogs in Africa. Next was yellow fever, hepatitis, and tetanus.

I called friends and asked them to collect my mail and to look in occasionally on the two houses for me while they harvested my plot of onions, carrots, and garlic.

I needed a new passport and ordered one right away when I realized that I didn't have many free pages and there could be a several month waiting period.

After many nights through April on the porch looking over itineraries and Lonely Planet guidebooks, I made up my mind; I would soon be hiking in the southern parts of Africa.

The month of May smothered the land with sticky heat and as May neared its end, I made arrangements to leave. On the first day of June I went online and bought a Greyhound Bus ticket.

Changes

Change rules the traveler and the traveler rules change. Freedom is the air that I breathe and the world seems like my back yard. My mother must have swaddled me in a Rand McNally bunting because a map brings me new life. Change is part of that excitement, new places, new people, new customs, new dress, new food, and new music. And the freedom to change itineraries is at the heart of it all.

I leaned back in my seat on the bus and watched as Missouri sped by the window. I thought back to those nights on the porch of the old farmhouse when I planned my trip to Africa.

As it turned out I did not need to worry about rabies, Africa had faded from my plans. For the next eight months I would take a very long bus ride. A drastic change of plans, yes, but this is the confession of a traveler and that is what a traveler does; a traveler is free to change plans at any moment.

I would leave the hot winds of Springfield behind me and travel for the better part of the next year but I would not be going to Africa; I would instead head south and take an extended trip aboard countless local and long-haul buses on an eight-month tour of South America. I vowed to head inexorably south and I would not stop until the roads ran out.

Indeed the roads did end at a dock in the southern reaches of Tierra del Fuego. I kept on south by boat, however, and fulfilled the dream of every traveler; I planted my hiking boots on new turf.

No turf crunched beneath my boots on landing, however; I found only icebergs. Antarctica's treasured stamp on my passport would elude me, at the southern end of my journey, only the penguins greeted me and they had no customs inspector.

South

The first leg of the trip was one I had made many times, a non-stop, 22-hour bus ride from my hometown of Springfield, Missouri to the Mexican border at McAllen, Texas.

In Springfield I hefted my pack into the luggage bay beneath the leaping Greyhound and was happy to shed the pack's forty pounds.

Taking my seat, I couldn't help but wonder if I had forgotten anything: two changes of clothes, three pairs of cotton socks, a linen shirt, Basque hiking boots, walking shoes, North Face tent, a sleeping bag, and pad. Over my shoulder, I had a carry bag with a heavy flannel shirt that would save me from the cold mountain passes and the frigid air conditioning systems aboard the buses, a serious problem it turned out in Venezuela and Brazil.

Day or night, it doesn't matter to me, I can doze on the bus and as long as I get out and stretch at each stop I can tolerate a long bus ride. The ride gives me time to read my lonely Planet Guide and plan the trip, although for me the trip is quiet linear; I go from stop to stop, bus to bus, city to city, until I get to an interesting city or village.

For some the long bus ride would be a hell of self-doubt, all that time to ruminate over past mistakes and what ifs and should haves. A teacher once told me that too much of that kind of thinking and you would be shoulding on yourself and I believe it. Life is short and meant to be lived in the moment, day spaces as one writer called it; life should not be lived in the past.

I reached the border at McAllen Texas without incident and left the bus to walk through the checkpoint where I filled out the tourist form, paid the 25 or so dollars, and was free to enter into Mexico.

Mexico

Now in *Reynosa*, Mexico, I boarded a long-haul bus that would run south along the Gulf of Mexico and stop in *Ciudad Victoria* where I could get an ADO Bus for Poza Rica. The bus route was south down the 900-mile coast to the port city of Veracruz on the Gulf of Mexico.

I had made this trip before. On previous trips I stopped to see the huge Olmec heads at the Jalapa museum, toured the ruin site of *El Tajin* with its Pyramid of the Niches, and detoured west to climb

El Taiin Pyramid Of The Niches. Veracruz

the Pyramid of the Sun at Teotihuacan.

On this trip I went south rapidly with Oaxaca City in my sights.

From Veracruz I caught an ADO bus bound inland over the mountains for Oaxaca, City, in total a 26-hour bus trip from the Texas border.

Coffee

I knew we were closing in on Oaxaca when we passed volcanic Mount Orizaba, the highest mountain in Mexico at 5610 meters (18,405 feet) and the third highest in North America.

Mount Orizaba is a snow-covered peak that harbors a year round glacier where extreme climbers come to practice climbing skills and train for expeditions to 20,320 foot Mt McKinley and 29,029 foot high Mount Everest in the Himalayas.

6

Nearby, the City of Cordoba was noted in my guidebook as the place were coffee first came to the new world, a plant now ubiquitous in Mexico but native to Africa.

I thought back three years earlier to the village of Pluma Hidalgo in the mountains of Oaxaca and the coffee plantation where I once visited.

Coffee farmer Lalo Marin had shown me, during that January visit, how he hung by a hemp rope on the edge of a steep slope in the coffee groves and manually twisted off the ripe fruit.

He was a tiny mountain man, perhaps just over a hundred pounds. Every pound of him was muscle, however, even his face flexed muscled dimples when he smiled, and he smiled often. Lalo loved to talk: talk about his farm, his coffee plants, and his burro Rayos who, during that visit, showed the mark of a vampire bat on the white fur of his neck.

Lalo shared his house with his dad and his wife and children on the top of the mountain with a view of a long strand of Pacific Coast beaches. The view included one of my favorite beaches, Zipolite.

He talked even as he placed the red fruit from the ten thousand plants on his ranch into the saddlebags slung over Rayo's back. After a morning of picking we went back to his house and he first sorted the berries by hand and then spread them out on a large patio to dry in the sun. He would rake these drying beans several times each day to encourage even drying.

After the beans dried properly he used a hand mortar and pestle that he made from a tree trunk to crush and remove the outer shell. Each berry yielded two green beans. When he had collected several bags of those beans, he loaded the bags onto Rayos and trudged down the mountain to the coffee collective in the village. At the collective the manager put the beans through a huller to further clean them and then he roasted the beans in a gas-fired oven.

One morning we brought some beans to the mill for roasting. The smell of roasting coffee filled the little village as the beans turned from green to rich brown. Lalo then bagged up the roasted beans and delivered them to the buyer for shipment to the market town of Pochutla on Oaxaca's Pacific Coast.

Later that morning Lalo served me fresh roasted coffee grown on his ranch and he served fried eggs from the half-wild chickens that roamed through his groves; the best I have ever tasted, served by a humble man who knows how to live for each day.

He was like so many of the people of Oaxaca who, regardless of difficult conditions, always have enough to share with visitors. He lived a simple life that made him a happy guy. He took what each day gave him and made all he could of his life.

These reminiscences had me looking forward to life's simple pleasures. I looked forward particularly to a cup of strong Oaxacan coffee at the El Jardin Zocalo Cafe in Oaxaca City.

Santo Domingo Church and Museum Oaxaca

Oaxaca

After nearly 48 hours on various buses, I finally reached Oaxaca City where I put in for what I hoped would be a few weeks rest.

I shouldered my pack and walked in Oaxaca's dazzling morning sunshine towards the pedestrian-only street, the Alcala. Between green stone buildings built in the 1600s I headed south on cobble streets for the center of town and the plaza called the Zocalo.

I never reached the Zocalo and my long awaited cup of El Jardin coffee, however; there was trouble in the streets of the city; a revolution had erupted and the fighting had spilled into the Zocalo.

I booked a room at the Santa Isabel Hostel, a place near the Soledad Church that was familiar to me. There I planned to stay for a while to rest and gather information from travelers coming up from the south.

Although I had planned an extended stay in Oaxaca City, since I have many acquaintances there, the trouble in the streets turned out to be an unruly teachers strike that developed into a riot. Fighting in the streets drove me out of town in a hurry.

According to the local papers, bands of revolutionaries, anarchists, communists, and hoodlums had joined a few thousand teachers and were battling police for control of downtown Oaxaca.

Roadblocks with overturned vehicles and burning buses were just a nuisance at first but when bullets began to fly and people started getting killed I wanted to leave Oaxaca.

I changed plans quickly and booked an early morning bus that left from the first class bus station and headed for Juchitan. From there I could get a bus to San Christobal de las Casas in Mexico's southern most State, Chiapas.

Chiapas State is certainly no stranger to revolutionary activity but the revolution in Chiapas had settled down a few years earlier so I planned to stay a few days. I left Oaxaca at 7 am on an OCC first class bus. Once on the road again I rechecked my possessions: ATM card, travelers checks amounting to $500, US $500 in 100-dollar bills, (easy to carry), and a Visa credit card. I spread this stash in several places on my person, hidden as best I could within inside pockets. In my front pocket, where I could reach it easily, I carried small bills in Pesos and some US dollars.

I felt now like I was on my way, Oaxaca being friendly turf, usually, fell far behind as I looked back at the hills ringing the colonial city and hoped that soon the trouble in the streets would end.

The bus cruised south out of Oaxaca's cluttered outskirts on route 190, the Pan American Highway. We soon entered a long valley between green spines of mountains that run the length of Oaxaca State. I could see the farmers in the fields as they coaxed oxen lashed to wooden plows that furrowed the rich alluvial soil made fertile by the first month of rainy season.

Further southeast in the valley, fields of blue maguey spread pointed leaves toward the sun to fill their pinos with sugar that would one day be baked to make Mezcal, the smoky distillate that precedes every Oaxacan meal.

Ahead I could see the distant mountains pinch in and loom green with a road winding up the mountainside to the south. The bus crept over the topes in the Mezcal village of Matatlan and then climbed into the mountains.

Switchbacks were our agonizing elevators to 9000 feet and then they conveyed us down again over the first of two mountain crests that stood along Oaxaca's Pacific Coast. We crept through twisting roads beneath stands of organ pipe cactus that stood on the hillsides like soldiers in formation.

Eventually the mountains leveled and we glided into the coastal plain of the Isthmus of Tehuantepec, the lowest landmass in Mexico between the two oceans. The Isthmus, with a peak elevation above sea level of only 750 feet, poses a stark contrast to the rest of Mexico's mountain vastness.

We moved across the plain while howling winds made the bus shudder and lightning pummeled the ground in the distance.

We reached Juchitan and from there I caught a bus headed southeast along the coast and then inland over the mountains towards San Cristobal de las Casas.

I hoped that the troubles in Oaxaca would soon resolve and that I could someday visit Lalo's coffee plantation on the mountainside in Pluma Hidalgo for a cup of his dark coffee and a plate of his wild eggs.

At that moment I planned to take what the day would give me and go where the highway would lead me. I continued south on highway 190 with my mind full of image of the Mayan people of San Cristobal de las Casas and their hand-made clothing and exotic customs.

I could never have imagined then, as I cruised south towards San Cristobal aboard an OCC Bus, that in the next two years not only would I swim in both the Antarctic and the Arctic Oceans, but I would walk with penguins, pan for gold, stare down a grizzly bear, and even find my self stranded in a town called Chicken.

> *I've touched, you know, incredible lands*
> *where, inside flowers,*
> *the eyes of panthers mingle with the skins of*
> *men!*
> *And rainbows bridle glaucous flocks*
> *beneath the rim of the sea!*
>
> *The Drunken Boat, Arthur Rimbaud*

" To see the world in a grain of sand, and to see heaven in a wild flower, hold infinity in the palm of your hands, and eternity in an hour.
William Blake

2. San Cristobal de las Casas

I had left Oaxaca City early in the morning because there were rumors that the protestors would set up roadblocks later in the day and the highway south would be closed. There were no morning buses to San Cristobal from Oaxaca City but from Juchitan I could book a first class bus to San Cristobal. I wanted to arrive in San Cristobal De Las Casas in the morning or early afternoon and have daylight to book a hostel. I wanted two nights in San Cristobal De Las Casas because I like the colonial town with its narrow side streets and town square and its indigenous markets.

San Cristobal de las Casas is an exotic place. The indigenous people dress in colorful clothing made by hand in their villages and they come to the old church dressed for socializing while they set up

13

the indigenous market. These predominantly Mayan people come streaming in from the countryside to sell every exotic handcraft and plant item imaginable including medicinal herbs.

The Santo Domingo market brings an excitement to the plaza. It is a treat to walk through the stalls and see all the unique wares for sale. The people in the market come from many different indigenous cultures that live in Chiapas and most still create by hand the goods that they sell.

In the morning, the mist hugs the rooftops around the market as San Cristobal shimmers in the rays of filtering sunlight. Wood fires in the stalls heat the breakfast tamales and send delicious scents hovering over the marketplace to tell you that San Cristobal is no ordinary place but a place truly different.

San Cristobal is perched on the edge of the Lacandon tropical forest in the high country that feeds the watershed of the Usumacinta River. The crossroads town has been for millennium a market town and way station for merchants who hauled goods from the coast bound for the ancient Mayan cities of Tonina, Bonampak, Yaxchilan, and Palenque. Earlier times would have seen Olmecs hauling shell and jade from their outposts at Izapa on the Pacific Coast 300 miles to their homeland of San Lorenzo Tenochtitlan in present-day Veracruz. The indigenous of Chiapas still speak Mayan languages: the Huastec, Yucatec, and the Western and Eastern Mayan. In San Cristobal de las Casas the dominant indigenous languages are the Western Mayan Tzeltal and Tzotzil.

Today San Cristobal is also a watering hole and way station for backpackers coming south from Oaxaca to the cascades of Agua Azul and for backpackers heading to the ruins of Tonina, Yaxchilan, Bonampak, Tikal, and Palenque, and for *viajeros* like me heading to Guatemala and points south.

Borders

From San Cristobal, I headed to Guatemala on a local bus and reached the lively border town of La Mesilla. From there the Pan American Highway, Route 190, took me to Guatemala City.

I passed through many borders in the following few months and at times they were crowded, at times deserted, and at other times unevenly regulated and amorphous. Here is where US dollars in small denominations and stashed in an easily reached pocket can come in handy. The dollar, God love its fading value, still has clout most anywhere in the world and they still recognize the US dollar even in the remotest village where people speak languages known only to a few. At the borders I could pay for the passport stamps with a few dollars in change if there was no money changer and I would be able to get the needed tourist visas.

Passport Stamp

I like the passport stamp, it can be a badge of courage not easily earned at some crossings but I like to get them nevertheless. The stamp becomes more than fancy when the authorities check your papers and look for the official stamp that tells them that you entered through an approved checkpoint and that you paid your visa fee. The passport stamp can also help you prove your whereabouts in case of a legal issue just as I once needed to do to refute a false charge on my credit card.

Once off the bus and in a strange city, I carry only a backpack and keep both hands free to fend off the unexpected. You never know when you will need both arms free to duck under low hanging trees, to steady yourself when dodging potholes, to get to your cash and papers, and to fend off the occasional petty thief.

Photos

I was planning to make photos along the way so I was carrying a Nikormat SLR that I have had for many years. This trip later proved too much for the venerable camera and it quit working near my campsite on Grey Glacier in Patagonia. I had a stash of 50 speed Fuji Velvia and 100-speed Provia and some Kodak 64 and 100 but I only had used half of the film when the camera went down. I later replaced it with a Canon digital Powershot model and the photos in these pages are a combination of the two.

Speeding Through Central America

I have backpacked through Central America so many times that on this trip I wanted to pass through as quickly as possible and spend my time in South America. Therefore, once I left San Cristobal, I planned to make a quick run through the Isthmus of Panama; I did not spend more than one night in any of the cities except Panama until I reached Columbia, South America.

The obsession to move can get so strong that I will endure much to be near the next bus station. Proof of this would be my digs in Guatemala. I checked in to the Paris Hotel, a faded place as old as they get with original furniture from a century ago. It is across from a bar that had hollering and music until three in the morning but I booked it regardless because it was two blocks from the bus station that would get me to the next city. I can put up with a lot of inconvenience if it gets me near the next bus.

Guatemala

I had time to shop a little in Guatemala. I picked up a watch for $1.50 USD because; up until then, I had no timepiece at all. This little watch served me well until it was later stolen from my backpack while I took a flight to Tobago, an incident that became a good reminder to lock my backpack and never carry anything that I couldn't live without.

Bus

I traveled from Guatemala City to the country of El Salvador where I stayed in the city of San Salvador, arriving at night and leaving the next day. I have never seen so many buses in any city. Downtown San Salvador is packed with buses.

From there I crossed the border at El Amatillo and stayed on the bus to Tegucigalpa where I booked a hotel two blocks from the Tica Bus Station.

Tica Bus

On many backpack trips through Central America I have never found the buses crowded. I just show up and buy a ticket; I never make reservations. This lack of itinerary might not be to some traveler's liking and for them there is an option in Central America, a system called the Tica bus. These first class, cross-border buses take passengers through Central America using the same bus and drivers for the duration of the trip. The bus makes stops at hotels in the various countries while the drivers put up for the night along with the passengers. Starting in Tapachula, Chiapas, these buses are an option for travelers that make the trip south to Panama City. Tica Bus makes border crossings easy and safe.

Tegucigalpa

I like Tegucigalpa, It has an interesting central square, streets full of markets, and a road up a hill that leads to a nice park that overlooks the town.

I started to walk up the hill for an evening view when a man ran up to me and insisted that I not go up to the park alone at night, a kindness noted from a stranger in a world that is not always kind.

I sent some time watching the flight traffic at the Toncontin Airport in Teguchigalpa. The airport makes news as the second most dangerous airport in the world and when you see planes dropping down between low mountains for a landing amid busy streets just four miles from the center of the city you understand why. The airport was made safer by the removal of a hill on the approach path and a lengthening of the runway in 2007 but it still has one of the shortest international airport runways in the world.

Luxury Bus

In Tegucigalpa I reserved a seat on a luxury bus for the following morning, a futile attempt to enjoy a luxury ride it would prove.

The bus was scheduled to leave the station at seven in the morning. The luxury bus, the first luxury bus that I had ridden on since leaving Missouri, had an upper deck for sightseeing. The traditional seating on the upper tier offered a picture window view. On the lower tier the bus had reclining seats that turned into beds. They also served breakfast.

The day before traveling I booked a front seat on the upper deck and looked forward to enjoying a picture window view of Honduras on the way to Nicaragua.

That morning when I arrived at the station, however, the conductor would not give me the seat at the front. He gave me a seat on the upper deck but someone who had more clout or more money than I had would ride in my reserved front seat.

I put up a heated argument but in the end I realized that it was fruitless. I have learned in the past that a traveler must often roll with these pitches of the deck. When you are in a country foreign to you, your rights and privileges often depend on what your money and connections can buy. If you have neither, your only option is to be flexible.

Thieving Beginners

From Tegucigalpa I went on to cross into Nicaragua and then on to Managua where I spent the night.

Here I had a strange incident that reminded me to keep alert while walking the city streets. A man approached from the front and I could see from the corner of my eye, another one approaching from the side. The man coming towards me put his hand out to touch me. I grabbed his arm and pushed his hand aside while at the same time I jumped away. I then turned and faced the two men and demanded to know what they wanted. They quickly turned and seemed to fade away down the street like ghosts. I don't know what they were up to but I was thankful that I had both arms free.

I prepare for incidents like this although they rarely happen. It doesn't bother me when it does happen, its no big deal. You have to be hard-shelled as a prairie tortoise to make a backpacking trip like the one I was making, traveling alone through Central and South America, a place of frontier towns and at times, frontier justice. Some people can do a trip like this, some cannot or would prefer not to.

Most people who are robbed will get careless in a bus terminal or they will walk alone in a seamy area of the city. After you have done some backpack traveling, you get the feel for when someone is looking at you with robbery on their mind. For the most part, however, people all over the world are kind and helpful, just like the man who went out of his way to warn me about the park in Tegucigalpa.

Sure at times people call you names, "Whitey," or "Gringo," or worse, but the kind people who run up to you and warn you not to walk in certain parts of the city make up for the few bandits out there who prey on backpacking road warriors.

Soon enough I forgot all the mundane bus rides and the dicey streets of Central American cities as we sailed the islands of San Blas and dined with a Kuna Queen.

"Avoiding danger is no safer in the long run than outright exposure.
  Life is either a daring adventure or nothing."

Helen Keller

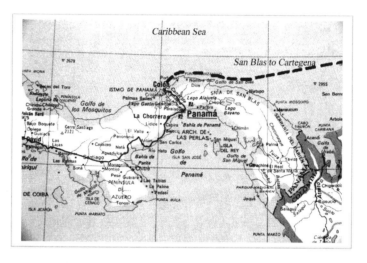

We sailed the islands of San Blas from Colon to Cartegena Colombia

"I know what I want.
I want it all.
I want to try everything once."
Anthony Bourdain,

"He gave the impression that very many cities had rubbed him smooth."
Graham Greene

3. Boat Passage

It is not so much the look of a hostel that gets me to visit but where the hostel is located that will seal the deal when I am racing through a country. I found just such a place in San Jose, Costa Rica, a hostel not so attractive but one just across from the bus station where I could get an early shot to Panama City.

Once in Panama City I put into the Prima Vera Hostel and started a search for boat passage through the Kuna Island of San Blas to Columbia. I was flexible in my plans and would head to any area of South America but I expected that most boats would be headed for Cartegena.

Boat travel was preferred at this leg of the trip because roads south of Panama through the Darien

Gap are relatively non-existent.

According to various reports, any travel in the Gap is dangerous. Over the years a few four wheelers have made the trip but several travelers through the Gap have been kidnapped and held for ransom.

The Darien Gap is just that, a gap in the Pan American Highway that runs from Prudhoe Bay in Alaska to Ushuaia in Argentina. The Gap is a ninety-mile stretch between Yaviza Panama and Turbo Colombia where there are no roads.

The land south of Panama City is mountainous terrain that then levels to river delta and swampland. The area has never been developed. The isthmus south of Panama City is 30 miles wide and ninety miles long. The roads resume in Columbia but the only safe way to get from Panama City to Columbia is by boat or air.

I wanted to go by boat so I checked other hostel bulletin boards and finally found a note from a German guy who knew a Frenchman who owned a sailboat. The French captain was taking paying passenger to Cartagena out of desperation; he had run out of money while on a world cruise.

I emailed the captain and then waited while I enjoyed Panama City. There was so much to do and see in the lively place. The life of the city seethes on Avenue Espania where you can find anything: hostels, gambling casinos, girls, music, and street food. There is just a lot going on.

You also find the cheapest taxis anywhere: $2.00 for any trip, even a 45-minute ride to the airport.

In the morning I caught a bus to the locks on the Panama Canal to watch the ships go through.

The normal sized boats go through in the morning and the supertankers go through in the afternoon. It is great watching the boats go through and imagining where they have been and where they are going, who is aboard, where do they come from, are they happy living every day at sea, what are their beliefs.

Welcome Aboard

The French sailboat captain responded via email after a day.

"Welcome aboard, meet at the docks near Colon in three days with all your luggage and we will leave."

When I arrived at the port near a Spanish stone fortress, I could see the boat anchored in the bay at

Portobello. I waved and soon realized that he saw
me when he hopped into an inflatable and headed
for the beach. Within minutes of our greeting, we
headed out to his sailboat. With hardly a flourish he
hauled anchor and me and three other passengers
were underway headed for Cartagena, Colombia via
the Archipelago de San Blas.

Pirates still roam the Caribbean and not the
movie kind. These boat owners all have weapons
aboard and although the captain never showed his, I
suspected that the former kitchen equipment
salesman from Paris was armed because I noticed
that one cabinet on the boat always remained
locked.

The trip was idyllic and I looked forward to a
relaxing 5-day cruise. Idyllic that is for the first two
hours.

I have been on the water before but I am no
sailor and had no idea when we set sail on the
glassy waters of Colon Bay that before long the
open ocean would turn our deck into such a frenzy
of pitching and heaving that I would wish to die.

Once we hit rough water I spent the rest of the
day and all of that night hanging over the side
puking. When there was nothing left to throw up, I
upchucked phlegm until I nearly dried up. The deck
would roll to the side and I swear the mast would
nearly smack the wave tops. Then the front of the
boat would suddenly lurch up and I would hang on
to the stainless steel rail with a death grip. Just as
quickly, the boat would pitch down and come
crashing into a wave with a shudder. By dawn there
was little left of me and I prayed for a merciful

death. As the sun rose, however, we came miraculously into the lee of an island and knifed through glass calm water. The captain dropped anchor in a sheltered cove.

I jumped into the jade lagoon with all my clothes on to clean up. I swam around the boat a few times trying to clean my shirt and within a few minutes, I couldn't believe it but I felt well enough to think about breakfast.

That dunk in the lagoon turned out to be a timely spiff up for me because later in the day we would be invited to dine with a Queen.

Date With The Kuna Queen

I came aboard after my dunk in the water with my clothes cleansed of the nights nausea. After a change of clothes I went ashore with the other passengers to the Island of El Porvenir to get a needed stamp to clear customs. The captain radioed for a meeting with the customs inspector and then we waited and waited some more.

Waiting gave us the opportunity to small talk and I learned a little about my fellow passengers.

Four of us had started the trip, five including the captain. We lost one who headed back to Panama via the small airport on El Porvenir. The captain, in his early 60s, had forsaken the life of a businessman in Paris to sail around the world. He had bogged down in Panama City and was gathering resources by taking passengers to Columbia so he could continue his world cruise.

We also had a German guy, a guy from Holland, and a Canadian. They were all backpackers in their

27

late 20s who, like many travelers, had an obsession to roam the world.

One had a wealthy family, another barely scraped by to fund his travels, another taught English. They were the same as all travelers who want to see the world: some meeting friends along the way, some volunteering, some learning about the world, some teaching language, others teaching composting, most doing anything to make expenses while they tour the world.

I saw myself in their faces; 40 years ago that was me, lured by exotic places and the chance to meet new people, see new flora and fauna, and to try new foods. Travel had been an obsession with me then and still is. Above all else, at the top of my list was adventure.

Once we had our custom stamp, we returned to the boat to sail on. We soon arrived at an idyllic island with a reef where we entered a sheltered cove and anchored in an azure lagoon. We fished and snorkeled on the reefs and then I went ashore to pick coconuts. By the time I returned to the boat, the Kuna Indians had come out in dugout canoes and offered their handmade textiles, fish, fruit, crabs, lobsters, and coco loco, a coconut drink fortified with a shot of rum.

A beautiful Kuna woman was among the men and it seemed that sunrays followed her as she moved. Her eyebrows were busy birds that fluttered with questions, dived with demands, and hovered with approval. With every tilt of her head or twist of her body she directed the men in a concert of impromptu commerce. She was the maestra leading the ensemble with every movement of her expressive body and animated face.

She was lovely and compelling to watch as she spoke to the men with authority one minute and kindness the next. Although theirs was not a matriarchal society as far as I knew, she left no doubt that she controlled the group of men. She invited us ashore for dinner in impeccable English and instructed us to bring the rum.

Dining With The Kuna Queen

By all means when the queen of any island invites you to dinner you put on your finest duds, even if it is a sun-bleached silk shirt and khaki shorts, and you show up on time. Late in the afternoon the captain opened that locked cabinet and out came not guns as I suspected but a bottle of rum. We piled into the inflatable and hauled up on shore where the Kuna Queen greeted us and led the way to her palm frond castle. She bid us sit at a log table as she served us a seafood stew with fish and crab. The bisque would have made the chef for the Queen of England envious.

We stayed late, talking and drinking coco loco well into the night as I fell for this Kuna Queen and her little slice of paradise.

We staggered into the inflatable in the dark of the early morning and then returned to the sailboat. Around noon of the following day we woke to no tourists and no other boats in sight. We went ashore again. No sign of the queen but I had a good look at the Kuna's palm houses made of woven cane walls and palm branch roofs. These people truly lived for the day, the hour, the minute I realized. If a storm should come and blow the straw hut away, they would just gather more palm and build their house anew.

In the afternoon, Kuna boats gouged out of huge trees came in from the open sea to bring fish and produce for sale. They pulled alongside our sailboat just like sea-born delivery trucks. Each time we met a group of men they would ask us if we had some rice or beans, coffee, or cigarettes. Although the sea provided all their needs, they craved foods common to us but not available to these island dwellers who harvested the sea. Coffee, cigarettes, and beans were exotics to the Kuna.

By now I was warming to this experience of touring the San Blas Archipelago. Of the 350 or so Islands in the San Blas Archipelago only 43 are inhabited by the Kuna; most islands do not have enough water to sustain a settlement.

We visited several of the larger islands and although my first day had been misery, the $250 that the boat passage to Colombia cost started to look like a bargain. Each afternoon we dropped anchor in a secluded cove to fish and beach comb We sailed among the islands for three days.

Paradise faded in the sunset as we picked up a breeze and headed across open water to Cartagena. With me dreading another siege of seasickness, the winds cooled and pushed us gently away from Eden towards the unknown. Then the winds slackened and the heat rose.

Running Aground

I could still see the clouds hugging the Khuna archipelago of San Blass as we entered the open ocean and I was relieved to see a glassy surface off into infinity with no storm clouds in sight. Then the wind all but died and we were forced to use the motor. We lugged slowly south as the heat became oppressive. Soon I was wishing for the cooling palapas of the Kuna and a repeat dinner with the queen.

During the afternoon of our fifth day on the boat the skyline of Cartegena came into view, a beautiful sight indeed until we got close. We headed for the channel into the harbor but failed to reach it before darkness came. With a shudder we ran aground on a sandbar offshore. In the blackness of night our keel remained pinioned on the edge of the channel in the unbearable heat while the captain vainly tried to re-float. After several hours passed the captain sent two of us ashore in the spare inflatable to lighten the load while he remained and tried to free the boat. We rowed into port guided by the lights of the city.

No customs inspectors met us in this one-time haven for smugglers, just oppressive heat and humidity. We tied up the inflatable at the marina as the Captain had instructed and then we went into the city to find lodging. It wasn't until the second day ashore that I went to customs for my passport stamp and official welcome to Cartagena de Indias.

Cartagena

I spent a day at the old walled town built by the Spanish in 1533. At the harbor a fort once defended the city from pirates. Balconies overhang the narrow pedestrian streets with many sidewalk cafes and many tourists. The heat and humidity, far worse than what I had fled in Missouri, was oppressive in the city but I booked a room for two nights because, although I had seen the city many times before, I always loved the history and romance, the architecture, and the friendly people of Cartagena.

I was now in South America, my goal, and I could slow down. Although my true goal was Brazil, I wanted to cross Venezuela and try to find a boat to Tobago to see where the steel drums got their start.

For two days I enjoyed the great street food in Cartagena, chicken, sausage, great bread, and lemonade, cold and refreshing fruit drinks. For lunch or dinner I would find a stand near a shady spot and dine.

For a splurge one of the mornings I went to the Charlestown Cartagena were a sumptuous breakfast cost $20. Expensive, yes, but a nice treat. The Charlestown Cartagena serves an endless cup of coffee, lots of fruit, and the morning paper in many languages including USA today and The Wall Street Journal. The newsstand price for those two papers alone in expensive Cartagena would nearly cover my breakfast so with the bottomless cup of coffee and several papers to read, I considered the price of breakfast at the Charlestown Cartagena a bargain.

From the City of Cartagena, I headed to Santa Marta, Colombia, Parque National Tayrona, a 15,000-hectare Jungle preserve that borders the coast of the Caribbean. I left the bus and walked to the entrance of the park to sign in with the guard. From the guard building I walked three quarters of a day on a dirt path through tropical jungle and coconut palms to the beach. At the beach they rent a hammock that you sling between trees by the shore. I planned to stay at the park for two days.

The Tairona Beach Park is named after the pre-Columbian Indians who built a city further east. The beach seemed endless, with palm trees leaning out over the water. And those waters are exquisite but the rip currents are fierce. Nobody swims there except at the beach called La Piscina.

I met two young men and a woman from Medellin. The kind trio didn't want me to be by myself there for my safety so they invited me to string my hammock near theirs. I strung the hammock between the palms and we sat by the fire talking. The wind came up a little and the men warned me to keep an eye on the wind; coconuts might fall if the wind came up too much.

I slept fitfully because I could hear the wind speed increasing and the trees all around me swaying. I couldn't stop thinking about falling coconuts.

Suddenly a crashing noise woke me with a start as something came smashing down on my hammock. I was sure I was a dead man from a fallen coconut. When I looked down I realized that the wind had ripped a palm frond from the tree and it was now draped across my legs. Sleep would elude me until the magic of sunrise made the long night of fitful sleep all worthwhile.

I spent three days at the park, hiking in the jungle, looking at birds and the howler monkeys, beachcombing, visiting with people on the beach, and dodging coconuts. Each night the trio and I, joined by other backpackers, lit a fire on the beach and sat around talking and drinking a little rum mixed with sweet coconut milk.

Such freedom seems elusive in the modern world so I cherished it. Soon I would nearly loose my freedom to the Venezuelan police.

Lost City

I left the park and walked back out to the highway where I flagged down the bus and headed to Santa Marta where I spent two nights. Good fruit drinks and skewers of pork cooked on a charcoal fire kept me happy. From Santa Marta, travelers book a five-day jungle trip to the ruins of Ciudad Perdida, the lost city of the Tairona culture.

I learned that on that trip you need to proceed with extreme caution. It is only recently that groups could go in there at all because of rebel activity. Someday I will risk this trip but at that moment, I had Riohacha and the border of Venezuela in sight. From there I went through Venezuelan custom and on to Maricaibo and from there to Caracas.

Caracas

It was my first time in Caracas and although I

stayed for two days I didn't enjoy the expensive city with a great deal of poverty. Many of the city dwellers are desperate and dangerous. The despair makes the city unsafe to walk at night. I left Caracas for Rio Caribe where I planned to catch a boat to Trinidad. On the way there I had a run in with the Venezuelan military.

I've seen thunderstruck archipelagos! and islands
that open delirious skies for wanderers:
Are these bottomless nights your nest of exile,
O millions of gold birds, O Force to come?
True, I've cried too much! Dawns are harrowing.
All moons are cruel and all suns, bitter:
acrid love puffs me up with drunken slowness.
Let my keel burst! Give me to the sea!

The Drunken Boat, Arthur Rimbaud
Rebecca Seiferle translation

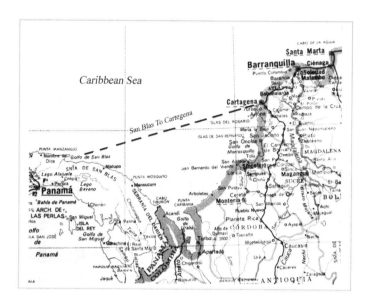

"I saw in their eyes something I was to see over and over in every part of the nation- a burning desire to go, to move, to get under way, anyplace, away from any Here. They spoke quietly of how they wanted to go someday, to move about, free and unanchored, not toward something but away from something. I saw this look and heard this yearning everywhere in every states I visited. Nearly every American hungers to move."

John Steinbeck, *Travels with Charley: In Search of America*

"Our battered suitcases were piled on the sidewalk again; we had longer ways to go. But no matter, the road is life." - Jack Kerouac

4. Venezuela

Venezuela Welcome

Call it the Venezuelan welcome if you wish or is it just a welcome reserved for gringos of the American, that is, the US persuasion.

We were pulled over at a roadside checkpoint and I felt the old bus groan as the official ascended the steps. In the back-light through the windshield I could see the silhouette of the ominous figure in the aisle. He looked like overfed evil searching for someone to punish.

His shiny, mid-thigh boots moved slowly down the aisle while I looked up only to have his evil eyes settle on mine. I lowered my eyes so as not to stare but could still see his excess flesh strain at the buttons of his tan uniform. No neck supported a head that just seemed to bulge from his shoulders.

He looked at me again with eyes that were slits laced across puffy, pock marked cheeks. He took another step closer and then with hardly a look to

37

the other passengers, all locals, he pointed at me with the exaggerated authority that a badge bestows on otherwise powerless people. With a grunt of contempt he motioned me out of my seat and out of the bus.

The bus waited while the officer went through every nook and cranny of my pack. Sweat poured down his brow as his disappointment grew at finding nothing. I feared a strip search was coming next but by this time most of the passengers had filed out of the bus and they gathered around and grumbled their annoyance at being delayed by this too-thorough military cop.

I just kept my mouth shut as he opened everything I had. He opened the tent, sleeping bag, he opened film canisters and threw them on the ground; he went through my shaving kit, everything. It was the most severe search that I have ever had and it reinforced an important lesson, never ever carry the slightest illegal substance or you could end up in jail.

I know I was singled out, because once he stopped at my seat and pulled me off the bus he never even looked at the rest of the passengers.

At times fake cops will come up to you and ask for your papers, particularly in Caracas where they ask for your passport and try to extort money, but this guy was the real deal and he was thorough and quite perturbed when he found nothing.

I have been taking long road trips for years, been attacked, been searched a dozen times, and even once was kidnapped, but I never went through a search like that. In retrospect, my many road experiences probably helped me keep my cool through this one.

I don't let this type of thing bother me, however, it is part of the deal when you travel in third world countries. I felt that this was just an inconvenience both for me and for the other bus passengers. Once the official was done, we got back on the bus and, before long, it was forgotten. I learned a long time ago in India to let things like this go, otherwise they eat on you and cause you pain, worry, fear, and anger, all negative feelings that can cause health problems. Easily said, but a philosophy that takes some practice.

So many reasons come into play for a search like the one I went through: the guy is having a bad day, he has a quota, he is trying to cultivate a bribe, he is doing his job, he is showing off his power to his fellow countrymen, he is bored, he is anti-US. Moral of the story, don't carry contraband. If you must have it, buy it on the spot and use it at the point of purchase, don't transport it.

Giuria

Once clear of the security check, we headed for a peninsula that is not far from Trinidad. There we would get a ferry from the port of Giuria and make a three and a half-hour boat trip to Trinidad's Port of Spain.

Along the way we had a breakdown and had to change buses. On the next bus, I took a seat beside a young woman and had a pleasant conversation as we rode through the tropical countryside. She was from a small town in Venezuela and she spoke

English well enough to enjoy practicing her language skills with me.

Like me she was heading for Trinidad and had booked a room at a hostel near where she would get the boat. She offered me space for the night in her room. I took the offer.

There is a fraternity out there among backpackers. People get out on the road for a long time and they meet other backpackers who provide company. People just don't want to be alone all the time. There is a camaraderie among the fraternity and shared pleasure and, at times, shared pain. In some areas, security is at the top of the list. Hooking up with others provides security for a while. Safety in numbers comes with joining others. This can also be a money saver: rides in taxis, guided tours of ruins, rides on boats; all can be shared and savings can result.

Most backpackers you meet are going along the same route that you are. You know that somewhere down the road you will meet again. The backpacker grapevine is helpful too; it provides conversation and good information about the places ahead. All people have to do is gain your trust and begin to trust you. Once trust is established there is no telling what will happen.

We arrived at her hostel at two in the morning and the manager said we had arrived too late, there were no rooms left. With no option, we headed back to town via the taxi, paying twice the price. We were lucky to find a posada located in a private home and flopped for the night.

We woke early the next day to rain. We headed for the dock to book a boat for Trinidad but chaos greeted us at the ticket office. A mob of ticket buyers surged around us. We fought our way to the ticket seller and tried to get a seat on the boat but we never got one. The boat left and we headed back to the posada where we hoped for better luck in the morning.

The next morning the young woman and I arrived at the boat dock early but were confronted again with a huge line. We took our place and settled in for a long wait. When I saw the price schedule I realized that with the posada expense, taxi fare, and a boat price higher than what I had been told, I might need more money.

The woman agreed to hold my place while I headed for the ATM. I left my pack at the house of the family where we had stayed and they promised to watch it.

I found the ATM but it would not dispense money. I went into the bank and presented ID and filled out papers. I paid a fee and did get money after a long wait. I then left the bank and headed to the house to get my pack. When I picked up the backpack a ton of roaches jumped out and scurried in all directions. Zillions of Palmetto bugs leaped from every compartment it seemed. I had to empty everything out to get rid of them. I then headed for the dock but by the time I got back to the boat the young woman was already aboard and I had lost my space in line.

I, along with other passengers, complained and begged and demanded that they provide a second boat. Finally they relented and brought up a local fishing boat. Twelve of us went aboard after the official checked us through immigration. As it turned out, with fewer passengers to check, we actually left for Trinidad before the first boat had left the dock.

After a three-hour trip across the bay, we arrived at Trinidad and entered a harbor full of luxury yachts. They shunted us to a dock further down the harbor away from the luxury marina and then they held us on the boat while we waited for Trinidad immigration inspectors.

It was ten hours before the official arrived and then he searched every suitcase so thoroughly that it took fourteen hours before I left the boat. By that time I had befriended an English backpacker on his way to Tobago where he would get a plane back to the UK. Now, two in the morning, we were clear of customs but there were no taxis available. When one did arrive, the driver wanted $35 for a ride to town. We refused and went out to the road where we flagged a taxi down and for three dollars he took us directly to the ferry for Tobago.

Security there wouldn't let us board, for them it was too early in the morning. In desperation, the Brit and I headed for a nearby Kentucky Fried and hole up for the night while we tried to ignore the locals who pestered us all the rest of the night begging for money or cigarettes.

At first light we went to the ferry but could not get on. It was a mad house with hundreds of people trying to get on a ferry that held only sixty. The lady tending the ticket booth assured us that we could get a ticket so we stayed in line but before we moved much closer to the booth, the ferry left without us. In desperation, we caught a cab to the airport and booked a flight to Tobago.

That was one miserable stretch of bad luck and it continued when someone handling airport luggage stole my $1.50 watch. I didn't lament that cheap little watch but I sure hated to squander so much time waiting in vain for that ferry.

Steel Drums

We finally reached Tobago and found it to be a beautiful Island. My sights were fixed on Bucco where the steel drums originated. The English traveler and I parted at the airport where he would catch a plane back to the UK. From the airport I hitchhiked to Bucco to spend the night.

Every Sunday in Bucco they hold a concert with live, steel-drum bands. People from all over the world attend. Virgin Airlines flies in a 747, an Airbus comes in from BOAC, at least four big planes had come in for the concert and were parked on the tarmac at Crown Point Airport.

Steel drum bands were on every corner and in every park it seemed and on Sunday night, a full orchestra composed of steel drums played for three hours.

I stayed three days in Bucco after I booked a room in a private home that I found through a tip from a local guy. At $12 per night, I had a private room with kitchen and bath.

Swimming and snorkeling on the renowned Bucco reefs and the Bucco Marine Park occupied my time. The Island is a paradise of white sand beaches and coral reefs full of incredibly colorful fish. I felt enticed to stay for weeks. Some day I will go back there but after three days of mornings snorkeling the reefs and afternoons of resting in a hammock and reading, I was itching to get to Brazil.

From Bucco I caught a plane to Georgetown, Guyana and landed at Cheddi Jagan International Airport. As we approached Georgetown from the air I could see the many rivers draining the plush interior. Guyana is noted for protecting its tropical forests; a reputed 70 percent of the forest are pristine and these parks make desirable places for tourist on eco tours to go trekking into the basin of the Amazon.

Georgetown, Guyana,

The Georgetown airport is thirty miles outside of town. The only way in was to pile into a collective van jammed with people, some hanging out the windows. The cab dumped us out at a huge building open to the sun with a tall, red clock tower. The area around the building was teeming with people shopping at the Stabroek Market

Walking through Georgetown during the day with people everywhere seemed safe enough but as I left my hotel in the evening the owner stopped me with a warning, "You would be a fool to go out at night in Georgetown."

I thanked him for the advice but I did go out to dinner. I made sure not to stray too far from the hotel, however, and I stayed in the lighted areas.

Georgetown was once part of a Dutch colony that later became British Guyana. The country achieved independence in 1996. The residents today, who live mainly along the coast near Georgetown, are 40 percent west Indian of Tamil and Telugu roots and 30 percent descendants of black African slaves. The population numbers less than a million people and includes 10 percent indigenous natives of several different tribes. This ethnic mix produces some interesting food choices in the street stalls and restaurants.

The City of Georgetown, however, seemed mostly black and mostly poor and with all the warnings about crime, I didn't care to see more of the city; I just wanted to get to Brazil.

Another Day In Georgetown

Next day I headed for the collective taxi stand to find a ride to Surinam.

Poor is an understatement for Georgetown; on the way to the cab stand I had panhandlers aggressively pushing me and demanding money.

When I reached the taxi stand, again things seemed desperate. Collective cab drivers were pulling me and pushing me to their cabs. Two guys then started a fistfight over who would take me. I jumped into one cab and closed the door while chaos ensued at the cab stand. I got out and tried to break up the fight between the two sinewy cab drivers who were wailing away at each other but when I nearly took a punch to the head myself I jumped back in the cab and closed the door again. The cab, half-full of passive black faces who had

45

seen this all too often, waited. After a half-hour, the dust settled and finally one more person came to fill the cab.

From there we roared out of the parking lot bound for Surinam with everybody acting as if it were just another routine day in Georgetown.

Guianas

These countries on the northeast edge of south America are called the Guianas. They include Guyana, Surinam, and Guyane, or French Guiana.

From Georgetown, I headed to Moleson Creek aboard the colectivo and went to the stilling or dock where I would go through immigration and board a boat to cross the Coientyne River to South Drain in Surinam. From there I took another collective taxi and passed through many dikes built by the Dutch along all the rivers that drain the Amazon Basin. We were headed to Paramaribo the capital of Surinam. At Paramaribo, I planned to slow down and visit for three days of relaxation.

Great architecture of Dutch design marks the city as different, the highlight, a 19th century Dutch wooden house, the Alberga, located on the prettiest street in predominantly white Paramaribo.

Tweety Fest

Paramaribo is situated on the banks of the Surinam River and can be blistering hot and humid. The friendly folks speaking English and Dutch, the colorful customs, and the unusual buildings, including a Muslim Mosque, however, make this a great town to visit. One other note of interest is the

Sunday festival, one that includes the most unusual contest I have ever seen.

They call it the Tweety Fest and it involves a domesticated bird called the Twa Twa, a finch that is resident in the jungle interior. This bird has such an unusual call that the men of the town, and a few of the women, keep these birds as pets. On Sunday they bring their birds to the park and convene to determine which of their birds has the loudest and prettiest song. The event is held on the Onafhankelijk square in an area of food stalls selling great foods of Asia and Indonesia.

Above the shouts of people ordering Roti, a pancake rolled with curries and stuffed with spiced lamb, the clatter of pots at Indonesian shops called Warungs, and the murmur of shoppers at Chinese food markets comes the cry of the Twa Twa. Dozens of the birds set up a cacophonous din as competition comes to head in the blistering heat of a Sunday afternoon.

French Guiana.

On the forth day, I left for an hour and a half trip to the Maroni River and to the border at Saint Laurent Du Maroni in French Guiana.

When entering a new country I get money from the ATM . At this border, I was surprised to receive Euros. I almost felt like I was in Europe but soon found that Cayenna French Guiana's downtown is nothing like Paris although they do speak French and it is costly.

The downtown is nice but not worth the forty dollars I paid for a crummy room. I spent the evening sitting in a French bar watching French TV, eating French fries, and drinking Pepsi made in France.

The architecture is not French Colonial nor is it European. Although they are stone buildings, they defy type.

Approuatue River

Next day I grabbed a colectivo and headed to St Georges del L'Oyapok on the Approuatue River. I went to the French police station but they were perplexed as to how to proceed. They saw few visitors from the USA and it seemed that border patrol was not part of the daily routine; they couldn't even find the passport stamp. After a few awkward moments of the officials rummaging through drawers they produced a stamp which one of the men applied to my passport.

I then boarded a small dugout canoe for a trip to Diapoque in Brazil. I was nearing Latitude 0 and the first leg of a long boat trip across the Amazon River.

If I desire any of the waters of Europe,
 it's the pond, black and cold, in the odor of evening,
where a child full of sorrow gets down on his knees
to launch a paper boat as frail as a May butterfly.

The Drunken Boat, Arthur Rimbaud
Rebecca Seiferle translation,

*"When you're traveling, you are what you are right there and then.
People don't have your past to hold against you. No yesterdays on the
road."* William Least Heat Moon, Blue Highways

5. Latitude Zero

Brazil, Amazon Crossing

On reaching Diapoque, Brazil, I headed to the
immigration office to show the yellow fever
inoculation papers. At this little border crossing, I
again changed money.

Any border in the world has an entrepreneur or
two with a fist full of bills who will change money.
Their rates can be a little less favorable than a
bank's but I always like to change to the currency as
I enter the next country. I change just enough to
cover any emergency that might pop up.

I also like to collect a few coins and have in my
collection coins from every country that I have
visited. I have hundreds of dollars worth of coins
from many countries stashed in a huge canvas bag
at the farm in Missouri that I break out now and
again to remind me of the many exotic places I have
visited.

I had finally arrived in Brazil and set out to enjoy it. I spent the whole day sampling food and touring the small town. I then went to the bus station and caught a bus to Macapa, Brazil, latitude zero, on the Equator.

Macapa, Anxiety At Latitude Zero

I had been on an all-night bus from the border of French Guiana to Macapa and arrived before dawn far from the city. I caught a local bus going into town and it took me to the square where I took another bus to the port to find passage across he Amazon Delta. Once at the docks I started to shop for a boat. I found one and bought the ticket. I had some time to kill so I put my backpack aboard and went into town to spend the day.

The boiling temperature and oppressive humidity forced me out on a point along the river where I found a breeze near the Fortalzeza de Sao Jose de Macapa, an old fort along the river. I poked around the fort and then towards noon I headed for the bus. My boat was scheduled to leave in mid afternoon.

Upon arriving at the dock, I was stunned to see the berth empty; my boat had already left. I stood dismayed until a guy shouted to me from the deck of another boat and told me that my boat had only gone for gas and would be back in an hour. That was a relief but because my pack was aboard it sure gave me a few moments of anxiety

River Crossing

Within an hour we were underway aboard a double-deck, wooden boat that would take 24 hours to cross the Amazon Estuary. They would serve us dinner and breakfast as part of the ticket price but our sleeping arrangement would be rustic at best. We were told to sling our hammocks on deck were ever we could. This was no luxury cruise.

In the alizarin blaze of an Amazon sunset we lugged through the maze of river channels that make up the Amazon Delta. We passed other boats coming and going in every direction. Boats of all description scooted out from adjoining streams and darted off towards all points.

After dinner everybody hung hammocks and before long there were hammocks wall to wall, bow to stern, port to starboard; the entire deck was a sea of hammocks. Seeing no room to string a hammock comfortably, I unfolded my pad and laid it on the deck.

I slept intermittently that night as we passed camps and settlements on shore, illuminated by their fires. The stillness of the river was fascinating, the profound silence broken only by the low chugging sounds that would announce another boat passing unseen in the dark Amazon night where the jungle seemed to gobble all the light. A voice would reach out from an unseen shore and the smell of cigarettes, or garlic, or diesel would be the only hint that other life was moving in the black night.

Sunrise sent a rim of gold over the forest of the Amazon estuary and then the light revealed a green jungle in every direction and a hundred islands in our path. We slowed and nosed into a bank where the crew extended a plank for new passengers to climb aboard. Underway in minutes with new souls aboard, we cruised between the islands where we passed sawmill villages by the hundreds.

At least every five miles on the banks there were lumber camps where workers were cutting the jungle into boards six feet long and eight inches wide. These rough-cut timbers were stacked in huge piles. I remembered the several hours in an internet cafe that I spent looking at Google Satellite maps of the huge Amazon River system and realized at that moment why the jungle along the river's course looked on the satellite maps like the bones of a fish picked clean. They were clear-cutting the forest. At that moment the brown color of the river in the estuary and the plume of brown that extended far out into the sea that I had seen on the satellite photos made sense to me. The clear cuts were allowing the rains to erode the land and much of Brazil was washing into the Amazon River and out to sea

At some sections of the river system, lumber camps occupied every mile of riverbank. As we chugged along we occasionally stopped in a camp town to pick up more passengers. With the hammocks taken up in the morning we had room for more passengers and the captain took every advantage to increase the tally. After one night and a full day, the boat was jammed with passengers and I was relieved to see the skyline of Belém. Steeples of colonial churches came in sight as we neared the dock in the old section of Belém, Brazil.

I jumped off the boat happy to be ashore in Brazil. I ran into the street looking for a local bus that would take me downtown. After looking at the map, I realized that the center was only two miles away so I walked to the middle of the old section of town and my hotel, the Fortaleza.

Belém
Belém revealed itself as I approached to be modern with a high-rise city center. The people-friendly city, the first place in South America, it turns out, to have pedestrian lights with a timing indicator showed its humanitarian side; pedestrians in Belém would need time and a warning when crossing the city's ultra wide streets.

In sophisticated Belém, Senior citizens ride buses free with a senior's card, and although I did not have one, I usually ducked the fare.

Mango trees line the streets of Belém and these trees are beautiful most of the year. When the fruit ripens, however, it drops constantly and you must take care. If the fruit comes down on your head it could do some damage.

Belém also pioneered the style of restaurant that charges your meal by the weight of the food on your plate. An innovation that has flourished.

Belém offered a stark contrast to the many undeveloped cities and villages that I had passed through in Central and South America.

Great fish markets selling salt water and fresh or brackish water fish and a farmers market also made the downtown interesting. I watched the women in the market who were gathered around huge sacks of Brazil nuts. Their job was to chip off the shell of the nut with a machete. With some quick strokes of the huge blade they were able to shell the nuts without damage to the meat within. They did all this without effort and incredibly they still had all their fingers.

Colonial buildings of Spanish design, rich in color, and an old fort on the river kept me busy between trips to Belém's great coffee shops.

What had built this once great colonial city I wondered; could it have been coffee, lumber, or even Brazil Nuts?

This appeared in the news a year after my trip

10 dead, 9 missing in Brazil shipwreck
Thu Feb 21, 3:07 PM ET

SAO PAULO, Brazil - A ferryboat carrying more than 100 passengers collided with a barge loaded with fuel tanks and sank to the bottom of the Amazon River on Thursday, officials said. At least 10 people died, and another nine were missing and feared dead.
The Almirante Monteiro capsized at dawn near the isolated Brazilian town of Itacoatiara in the jungle state of Amazonas, state fire spokesman Lt. Clovis Araujo said.

He said 92 people were rescued by several small boats and the state's floating police station, a 32-foot vessel that travels up and down the river and was in the
area at the time of the shipwreck. Rescue teams recovered the bodies of four children, five women and one man, Araujo said, and a check of the boat's passenger manifest indicated nine people were still missing.
"The chances of finding them alive are remote," he said. "We will keep searching until the last body is found.
He said he did not know how many people were on the barge, but "no one was hurt and the barge was not damaged."
Many of the missing were likely passengers who were asleep in cabins inside the two-story wooden vessel and were unable to get out before the boat sank, state public safety department spokesman Aguinaldo Rodrigues said.
"As far as we can tell, just about all the survivors were passengers sleeping in hammocks on the deck," Rodrigues said. Rodrigues said it was too early to determine the causes of the accident, but "visibility was very
poor" at the time of the collision during the lunar eclipse that began Wednesday night.
The survivors were taken to the small town of Novo Remanso and sheltered in the local church. They were to be taken by helicopter to the state capital of Manaus.

"When we get out of the glass bottle of our ego
and when we escape like the squirrels in the cage
of our personality and get into the forest again,
we shall shiver with cold and fright.
But things will happen to us so that we don't
know ourselves.
Cool, unlying life will rush in."

D. H. Lawrence

"When you travel, remember that a foreign country is not designed to make you comfortable. It is designed to make its own people comfortable."
Clifton Fadiman

6. Belém

Belém does have great coffee and that is partly what built the city. While rice, sugar and lumber have all been exports, the last great economic surge was due to the exporting of rubber.

Belém offered some of the best coffee shops and pastry shops that I found in all of my travels through Mexico, Central America, and South America. The pastry cakes were sweeter and more delicate than anywhere else on my trip. Mexico may have great breads but Belém has the finest pastries.

Belém is a modern city of high rises that also offered lots of good street food and some great markets on many of the streets. Lots of prostitutes filled the street as well.

In Belém I met many travelers who pass through this river crossroads going in all directions through South America. These travelers included three backpackers from England who were looking for any consumable herb. The British invented independent travel and I met the intrepid Brits all along the way.

Especially ragged and interesting in Belém were the fish markets and the docks. One of the harbors was jammed with colorful boats that were crammed into the small bay. Only about 100 yards on three sides, the fishing port was chock full of boats that were so closely packed that on ebb of the nine-foot tide, they would lean against each other as they lay in the mud. When the fishermen on board were working their boats and cleaning their catch they just disposed of the viscera right over the side and onto the water and eventually onto the mud. This smorgasbord of gory fish parts brewed a heck of a stink but it was sweet perfume to the vultures and scavenging wildlife that swooped in to clean it up.

The old section of Belém, first founded in 1616, is a texture filled assemblage of narrow cobble streets, decaying buildings, markets, and crowded sidewalks. The old section attracts tourists who walk to the old squares and to the colonial churches near the river.

Colonial buildings in many colors throughout Belém's downtown attracted me and I stayed in the city for five days.

While I was enjoying this antique ambiance, the buses going in every direction had me already planning my next bus trip.

Bus to Fortaleza

I wanted to leave Belém for the Atlantic Coast but it was not easy to get a handle on the long distance bus system that would take me to my next stop, Fortaleza, Brazil. This turned out to be a difficult trip.

I wanted to head south along the coast to see the beaches on the Atlantic Ocean north of Rio but getting there would take some doing. I would need to get a bus first to an intermediate city, then another bus, and then get a collective cab, or Combi, as shared taxis are called in Brazil. I would finally make Fortaleza, an ocean-side city located on the Atlantic and my first beach on the way to Rio, but it would be a struggle.

I did not find a quick trip from Fortaleza to Rio either; I walked the sands of many a beach on the way.

Beaches

That was OK with me because I love beaches.

Between Fortaleza and Rio there are many great beaches, several of which I had in my sights. I planned to pause were I could on my way south along the coast and anticipated a few extended stops at the more remarkable beaches.

Of these stops I included Recife, a high-rise beach resort town where I stayed for three days enjoying the great beaches and warm waters of the Atlantic.

Recife's old city is a big crumbling area with a wide river that barely moves. With that lack of movement comes a strong odor. Nevertheless, tour ships dock in Recife and tourists visit this center of Brazilian culture. The tourists usually stay in nearby Olinda, a town billed as the prettiest town in Brazil.

I visited Olinda and found preserved colonial buildings and cobble streets, grand old churches and a nice hill with a view of the city that made Olinda a pleasant but expensive visit. A few items in the laundry cost me $14 USD, an unexpected luxury scrubbing or was it a luxury drubbing.

In a nice park, I picked up the seeds of some plants, a hobby with me, a farmer at heart. I like to work with the seeds in my greenhouse back home or I will put the particularly attractive ones in a jar for a decoration in the kitchen.

I check with a botanist friend first and make sure there is no harm in planting the seeds. Most every plant from other climes that will grow in the US is already there he tells me. Cruise ships, cargo ships, container ships, and airplane freighters have spread the world's flora and fauna to all continents far more rapidly than I ever could.

I love a good beach as a place to rest. I get off the bus when I am tired and I like to rest at the beach where there is always music, ballgames, stickball, frizbee, surfing, and of course great food.

Brazil is a lively place. There is always a party on the streets and bands playing Samba. The bands also play the Latin beats that I have heard in Mexico but they play them with far more subtlety.

The people on the beaches were dark skinned people, a mix of Portuguese and black Africans with some indigenous native mixed in. These brown-skinned people were a fun-loving, music-loving bunch.

Lots of African style dress hinted at the strong African influence and, in fact, the African soul of Brazil is Salvador Bahia, a beach town where I spent a week.

Bahia Todos Los Santos,

On a peninsula at the mouth of the River Bahia Todos Santos, a steep bluff divides the city. The sections are called Bajia, at sea level and Alta, the town at the top. An elevator takes passengers between the upper city and lower city.

In the center of the city there are two big squares and that is where the history and nightlife happens. Pelourino Square is also the location of the San Francisco Church, a Baroque monument to excess.

The city had lots of wealth at one time and they poured a considerable part of that wealth into this very ornate Baroque church that had many statues of European-looking angels, pregnant angels at that.

I love to explore the street food and found a local favorite: acaraje, a brown-eyed pea or bean fritter stuffed with shrimp, onion, garlic, and a touch of cayenne and deep fried in palm oil. Another street food delicacy that I liked was pasteis, a deep-fried palm oil turnover filled with mixtures of meat, chicken, or cheese. These are treats of dubious health value but a backpacker walks off the extra fats.

Extremely steep hills divide the upper and lower city on the ocean while streets in the center hum with street music, beer joints, restaurants, and lots of shops selling art. The people were friendly, some brown skinned, some black, and some light skinned. The town also attracts many world tourists to give it a great diversity of people.

From Salvador I went to Puerto Seguro. There, a man told me that I should go to Arrail d Ajuda, a colonial town on the ocean that I needed to see. He told me to go to the end of the dock and get a ferry to Arrail d Ajuda and then get a combi to the square.

This turned out to be a good tip, as the village had a nice clean square and an area of quaint hotels and B&Bs, classic buildings surrounded by tropical trees and a unique architecture with no high-rise buildings. All of the roads were cobblestone and they ended at a beach lined with restaurants and hotels. I enjoyed a beer and some swimming at this upscale beach town. This was my last beach before Rio so I spent the day there and caught a ferry back in the afternoon, hoping to catch a bus South to Rio. This would be a long trip that I judged to be 36 - 40 hours.

Bus To Rio

Soon I was on a bus and on my way to Rio. I stopped the next day for a rest briefly and then caught another bus to continue to Rio.

By now my mind was full of images of the beaches that I had heard so much about: Ipanema and Copacabana. Soon I was moving south again towards Rio, normally a three-day trip by bus from Fortaleza. Of course, for a beach loving backpacker it turned into ten days before I heard the sambas, tasted the foods, and walked the powdery sands of Rio's Ipanema Beach.

Rio Vibes

Coming into Rio was quite impressive as the bus came over a huge bridge above the commercial port and I could see the cruise ships and the busy harbor; I love to look at boats of any kind.

The bus station was in a run-down part of the city but luckily I came in during the daytime. I left the bus and checked out the local buses as I looked for the bus to the Cococabana Beach. I caught what I thought was the bus but only reached an area of hotels within a few blocks of the beach. With luck it was near the hostel where I had planned to stay.

Bad Hostel

I walked the few blocks to my intended lodgings in Rio and went in the lobby but quickly felt a chill come over me. The help seemed harried and indifferent; they gave me and other clients no attention. They were ignoring the guests and the place just didn't feel right to me.

I depend on a friendly staff in the hostel for up-to-date local information but when a hostel gets huge or the staff gets over-worked, they get surly they just aren't friendly or helpful.

The bad feeling about the place centered on the indifference of the staff, too busy for me or the client that was ahead of me in line. The place was clean but it just didn't feel right. The girl at the desk was chatty alright but the problem was she had no time to chat with the customers who were waiting in line.

The dining room was unappealing also, it had the look of a NY City cafeteria, a sterile looking place without personality. That first impression hit me hard. I felt the staff would be just too busy or too indifferent to bother with clients. When the place doesn't feel right to me, I move on.

Good Hostel

Disappointed that the hostel had such a bad vibe, I went around the corner and luckily found a great hostel with everything I needed including a location just four blocks from Cococabana Beach. For eight dollars a night I had the whole dorm to myself for nine days, five beds to a dorm but no one else was there.

My instincts proved their worth on this occasion. I knew beforehand that there are at least ten hostels in Rio and as it turned out, the place I chose, run by a German lady for a local owner, was ideal. She gave me all the local info I needed and couldn't have been more helpful.

I stashed my pack and headed for Cococabana Beach, a place that I have heard about all my life. Sure enough the beach fulfilled all the fantasies, pretty girls in bikinis and thongs, dark skinned beauties prancing on the beach, a few topless; Cococabana just the way I had always imagined it.

Cococabana Beach

I walked Cococabana Beach for at least two miles, stopping at stands that sell food and sampling a beer and some coconut milk. All along the beach people were making elaborate sand sculptures and had set out small pots for donations. I spent the rest of the day checking out hotels and restaurants.

At my hostel I had changed into a blue short-sleeved cotton shirt and jeans with tennis shoes and baseball hat with no logo. I seemed to fit right in, as the dress of many in Rio was very similar it turned out.

I felt great about being in Rio, lots to do and the more I stayed the better I liked it. Surprising to me, it was not that expensive to eat in open front restaurants along the beach.

After all those bus rides I was tired of traveling so I relaxed and slept late each day. I ate good full meals and let everything catch up with me. When I did go out to see the city, the streets near the beaches occupied most of my time. I also rode the bus all over the city and had a good look at Rio's museums and culture. I also found some interesting rock faces that block some streets while others have tunnels and roadways through the high cliffs.

At one point I found myself at the foot of Rio's notorious Rocinha Hill favela, one of the shanty towns that seem to share space with high-rise luxury buildings. Luckily it was during the day.

In Rio you see the stark contrasts between rich and poor as four sections of the city are crammed with makeshift housing. These favelas have only partial services such as light, sewer, water, and rubbish removal. The housing is often box-like structures made of discarded wood and plastic tarp.

Visa

Early on, I applied for my visa to enter Paraguey. I like to get this done quickly and well ahead of my departure date so I found a bus to the embassy of Paraguay and headed there on my second day. For $60USD I received a visa good for the lifetime of my passport.

I like to get the visa for the next country as soon as I can and would rather not wait until the last minute. I wanted to be in Buenos Aires by the middle of December. This would allow me to hike in Argentina and Chile while avoiding the end of December, and January/February crowds of locals who take to the trails and campsites in the mountains of Argentina and Chile. This schedule caused me to limit my time in Rio and to make my arrangements on a timely basis.

Ipanema Beach

After I got the visa, I went to Ipanema Beach, a mile long strand with volleyball and lots of locals on the beach. Ipanema is lined with buildings and condos and capped by a huge rock at end of the beach. I walked the beach and sat on the rock to watch the sunset.

Ipanema had lots of vendors peddling homemade stuff along the beach, lots of hippies selling homemade jewelry, and mobile food stands. In this liberal society of Cariocas, as the locals call themselves, they seemed to allow most anything.

My daily thing was to go to the Copacabana Hotel for coffee and check out the excerpts from the newspapers of the world in a handout compiled by the hotel. I would get my coffee at the hotel coffee shop and sit with a view of the ocean and read the headlines from around the world culled from many international papers.

In between Copacabana and Ipanema beaches there were shops to visit and food stands to sample. I also liked to go to the dock and watch the boats.

On Sundays they close the street in front of Ipanema Beach and turn the street over to roller bladers, skate boarders and bicycle riders, with a few dog walkers and strollers mixed in.

I love to sample the world's metros and made many trips on Rio's metro. The Rio subway and metro bus system extends far into the suburbs. I took many subway rides in Rio and during one ride I spotted a poster about the orchid exposition at Rio's Botanical Gardens where they had hundreds of flowering orchids. I am an avid gardener so this exhibit became the highlight of my trip. Hundreds of flowering orchids throughout the park made it a great, day-long visit for me.

Next day I took a bus to the statue, Christ The Redeemer. This is something that I felt I must see on a visit to Rio. The cost was $35 for a cog train ride up the side of the rock to the top where Rio revealed itself through the mist. From high on this mountain I could see the sprawling and impressive city of Rio De Janeiro at my feet. A sign made it clear that there would be no refunds of the ticket price.

"We are not responsible for cloudy days," the sign read.

As we rose we came into the clouds and I feared my ticket price would be wasted when we passed through a misty rain. At the top, however, the clouds miraculously broke and Sugarloaf and Christ the Redeemer emerged from the mist as if on cue to give me a fantastic view and a memorable sight indeed.

For the rest of my stay in Rio I walked the town parks and visited the interesting buildings. I stayed in Rio for nine days and met many other backpackers. We would hook up and go out to dinner or go to the beach and the gambling casinos or walk the beach or the marina and look at the yachts and sailboats.

I loved Rio but after my nine days in the tropical heat my feet were ready to go south across the Tropic of Capricorn.

I would soon be in the cooler air south at Iguazu falls in the park known as Catarata, a nature preserve of 250 waterfalls.

"A good traveler has no fixed plans and is not intent on arriving."
- Lao Tzu

7. *Tropic of Capricorn*

Tropic of Capricorn
Rio is just north of the Tropic of Capricorn and this puts it just at the edge of the tropics. After my nine days in the tropical heat of Rio, I was ready for cooler temperatures. As I headed south the climate changed when I entered the temperate zone. I booked a bus that took me south towards Iguazu Falls and Parque Nacional do Iguacu, Brazil.

Africa
While on the bus ride to Iguazu I thought back to Rio and my original plan of going to Africa. It had been my intention to visit Africa during those days back in Missouri when I sat on my porch and first planned my trip.

I thought that I might get a ship from Rio that heads to Africa. When I searched, however, I couldn't find a passenger ship anywhere. There used to be a regular run of passenger ships but the only one I could find was a gay boat that left Rio on a regular run several times a year and docked in Cape Town, South Africa.

Cape Town is a beautiful city I understand from reading about it and I wanted to tour there but I decided to complete my tour of South America first and then look into a boat to Cape Town later. As events unfolded, however, I wrote it off as not possible on this trip.

Although I still want to see the great beaches along the African Coast, and I would also like to see Namibia, I would put it off for a later trip. During my bus ride I decided to stay on this side of the Atlantic and finish my tour of South America. I know that after I rest for six months back home on the farm I will get itchy feet again and will be hitting the road. Maybe Cape Town next year.

On the way to Iguazu Falls I passed through Sao Paulo as I crossed the Tropic of Capricorn. I was interested in the metro system of Sao Paulo, billed as one of the most modern of South America's Metros but at that time I had my fill of cities for the moment. I passed on a visit to Sao Paulo

The Metro

Metros interest me because of the underground life that they harbor.

Whole cities of sorts exist in the subterranean tubes of the metro. You find up-scale and trendy shops that exist on the same walkway where you find beggars, panhandlers, and thieves. They all coexist underground where all manner of man and beast mingle on the same terms. The metro makes every person equal for the moment; they pay the same fee, walk the same corridors, pass through the same turnstyles, and occupy the same rude seats. And as a bonus, the metro gets me to places quick and cheap while providing free entertainment.

I will get on a subway and ride it all day. On any subway there is also all kinds of advertising and posters, photo exhibits on the walls and often free entertainment. It is an unusual place the subway.

I have seen many of the world's metros: London, Buenos Aires, Rio, Paris, Munich, Mexico City, and New York. Someday I will ride the Moscow subway. I love the metro.

On the subway you must, of course, be careful or you will be the victim of a pickpocket. I stick my paper money in my sock; that is a safe enough place. If the subway is jam-packed, however, I avoid them.

I was once pick pocketed in Mexico City and although they only took twelve dollars from my front pocket, the incident left me cautious. A group of young people working as a team got the best of me that day on the Mexico city subway.

At first I felt violated but since the loss was minor I got over it quickly enough. It taught me a lesson, however, and now I keep my small change in a front pocket while I sew up my back pockets where I keep my larger stash. I open an access port reachable only by taking down my pants. Awkward yes but that way I never loose too much if the pickpockets, who often do work in groups, rob me, as they did on the Mexico City subway.

I don't like money belts so by secreting money and valuables in several places, I avoid the annoyance of a belt. I hide the bills in several pockets and avoid the agony of a large loss of money. In Mexico City I lost twelve bucks but the incident left my mind pretty quickly once I got up in the city and started sightseeing.

Igauzu Falls

My destination when I left Rio was the falls of Parque National Iguazu in Argentina and the Parque Nacional do Iguacu in Brazil. There are 250 separate falls in the parks and once I reached them I spent the whole day touring.

I bought a hostel card at the International Hostel on the Brazil side of the park at Albergue de Juventude Paudimar Hostel. That was a reference that I had found through my Lonely Planet.

For twenty dollars each, a guide took five of us to the park and left us for the day. He took us to a spot near the Igauzu River where we could see Paraguay and Argentina. The highlight of my trip that afternoon was the falls called the Devils Throat.

I stood on the edge of the falls and looked straight down to the Devils Throat. My feet were at the edge of the water and I looked into the mist as the water surged over the cliff and thundered into the gorge. I became mesmerized by the sight of the rushing water and I stood for an hour in the throat enjoying the many feelings that came to me.

Standing on the edge as I was, I could feel the power of nature. I felt a compulsion to jump, a strange thought indeed, but jumping off and spreading my arms like a bird would make me one with the birds and with the rushing waters. These were strong feelings to be sure but luckily only feelings that I would not act out.

Another sensation came that I enjoyed, the feeling of freedom. I saw it as the freedom of a traveler to stand on the edge of the world. If only I could be suspended over it and sail above it, if only I could become one with the rushing waters and preserve this light-headed rush that I felt from the power of the water and the deafening roar that vibrated through me.

These experiences are the reason that I travel, to experience new events powerful enough to produce a mental sensation as if my consciousness has left my body. I want to let my mind drift out over the falls and to look down from the outside and see my body floating in the mist. These were powerful images that I can still feel today.

My mind will take me right back to that day when I looked down the Devil's Throat, the day I got giddy and laughy, the day I turned to the person next to me and they were giddy and laughy. This is why I travel. Experiences like this are more powerful than any I might have at home where everything is familiar and safe and, yes, old.

Experience is why I travel, and why I travel to places like the falls. New places get my heart pumping and my blood rushing even if it just for an hour. The feeling of standing on the edge of the Devil's Throat will last for years; the memories of those falls will last a lifetime.

Wine Country

From the falls I went across Paraguay and took an all-night bus ride that stopped at a few stations on the way but had as its destination Asuncion, Paraguay.

This border crossing is notorious for masses of people trying to smuggle goods as they go through and attempt to avoid sales tax. I was a tourist heading to Argentina and had nothing to declare but I found myself in a huge line. There were no signs but after asking a few people what the deal was I discovered that it was the wrong line. It held me up for a few minutes but once I found the proper line I moved quickly through customs as other people were being nearly strip searched and detained for trying to smuggle consumer goods without paying the import duties.

I spent the night in Asuncion, the capital of Paraguay. I was just passing through the plains in the south, a region of rolling hills, on my way to Mendoza Argentina via Tucuaman.

From Tucuaman I went to Cordoba and I spent a day waiting for a bus in an interesting square with lots of activity. The city had a European-feel to it and I enjoyed it as I waited for a bus to Mendoza, the heart of Argentina's wine country.

Once I reached Mendoza, I checked into the Hostel International where I joined other backpackers from all over the world. They were mostly Europeans, which included, of course, the inventors of travel, the British. These travelers were ensconced in Mendoza for some serious wine tasting.

The British travelers are everywhere in the world and they are brave and intrepid. I am sure if I was flying off the edge of the Devil's Throat Falls there would be an Englishman flying beside me. In Mendoza the streets are lined with sycamores that form tunnel like borders of foliage, much like the roads in Provence. Like Provence and all of France, this region is now producing some great wines. Spanish speaking but northern European in feeling, the city has its own ambiance and it is not necessarily European.

Great cheese shops and great bread shops, beautiful parks and plazas with tiled sidewalks, and shade trees on the avenues make this region different.

While in Mendoza I visited the bread shops to buy small loafs of bread. From there I would go to the cheese shops to buy a cheddar, and then to the wine shops to buy a bottle of red wine such as a Malbec and Merlot blend that they labeled, Malbec/Merlot. I then would go to one of the parks shaded by sycamores for a picnic. I spent three days in Mendoza enjoying the wines and breads and their fine chocolates.

Mendoza Wines

The good wines in the area cost about five dollars a bottle and with the great weather in October, early Spring in the southern hemisphere with warm days and cool nights, I could picnic with bread, wine, and cheese almost anywhere. The nights became cooler as I moved south even in what

is their mid summer, a season which includes
December and January.

Mendoza is noted also for its chocolate. The
stores feature candy animals, chocolate bars, and
candy treats of all kinds made with chocolate.

On my fourth day in Mendoza, after sampling
many types of chocolate, I caught a bus headed to
Santiago Chile.

River in Chile near Puerto Montt

Santiago Chile

Bearing west out of Mendoza, I crossed the Andean
Cordillera, which includes some of the worlds
tallest mountains. This range includes the tallest
mountain in the Western Hemisphere, 22,837 foot
Mount Aconcagua. (6,960.8 m)

Chile wine region

On the Alta Montana Route we had a magnificent ride over the mountains and then we crossed the border between Argentina and Chile. Oddly enough we did this crossing in a tunnel.

The tunnel through a mountain had a large underground chamber that included an immigration stop. The customs area was a huge subterranean vault where they checked everything in the luggage.

The inspectors were looking for goods that people try to smuggle to avoid sales tax, goods such as electronics and textiles.

In an attempt to avoid the required duty payment, passengers had children's shoes tucked up under their dresses, computer gear stuffed in their shoulder bags, and textiles wrapped around their bodies. I had nothing to declare so I breezed through but some passengers had their luggage confiscated and where required to pay a duty payment to retrieve it.

This crossing was the most heavily policed. Although I crossed the border between these two countries many times on the rest of the trip south, most crossing were easy.

The bus crested the mountain and we entered Santiago where we were surrounded on three sides by snow-capped peaks that had my heart longing for a hike in the mountains of Patagonia.

8. Santiago, Chile

I had long looked forward to visiting Santiago Chile, a city I had read much about. Chile itself always sounded exotic and exciting, especially the Island chain that runs down the western coast of Chile to Punta Arenas.

Santiago at 1,700 feet above sea level occupies a broad valley surrounded by the towering, snow capped, Andes Mountains. The city was founded as a Spanish colony in 1541 after battles with the resident Incas and soon became the capital city of Chile.

I left the bus and headed for the modern metro station where I took a train to Londres, a bohemian area of universities with lots of bars, shops, and old buildings. I was looking for an old house open to backpackers called Residential Londres, it was there that I wanted to stay.

Of course I had not made reservation, preferring to keep my travels spontaneous, but knowing that, at times, impromptu travel will cause me grief. And sure enough, when I arrived at the hostel it was full.

The staff told me about a private home nearby where I was able to get a bed in a dorm. I moved in to the eight-bed, nine dollar a night dorm room, vacant but for me. I unpacked with plans to spend a few days.

One of the tenants in another room was a black man from South Africa. I asked him many questions about his country, still keeping Africa in my long-term plans.

"Avoid Johannesburg," He said, "But anywhere else is safe and interesting."

He and I went to dinner and we talked about many places of interest including Easter Island. Next day I started to formulate plans for a trip to Easter Island.

Jacaranda

The streets of Santiago are lined with jacaranda and they were in full bloom. That made Santiago a magic place of old brick and stone buildings shaded by lavender colored trees. All that beauty coupled with a great location has caused Santiago to become an art and culture capital. Santiago offers its residents a few hours drive to the Pacific Coast beaches and a few hours drive to the Andean ski resorts.

I learned the modern metro quickly and it became a great resource to get me around Santiago.

On my list of wants was a day or two of sampling Chilean wines. I found some great wine stores where I could buy a bottle of white or red, go nearby for cheese, and then to the bakery for fresh bread. This was my lunch on several days while I toured the city.

A huge stone church in Baroque style occupies a square with pedestrian streets in all directions off the square. These streets are full of high-class shops and interesting espresso shops where women in revealing outfits serve you a shot of espresso and not much else but a view. The streets were full of friendly people and many local residents spoke English in predominantly Spanish-speaking Santiago.

I stayed for five days in Santiago while I toured the city. Santiago offered sightseeing in the farmers markets, fish markets, fish restaurants, and of course the espresso shops. Great architecture and shady, tree-lined, pedestrian streets made Santiago a tourist friendly town. Lots of pretty girls and the Mapocho River that comes cold out of the Andes and rushes right through the middle of town beneath bridges made Santiago different and interesting.

Food

Santiago's food interested me especially the meat dishes served in the parrilladas, the Chilean barbecue restaurants where meat grilles near or at the table. Another favorite dish was the lomito, gobs of sliced pork and avocado stuffed into a sliced baguette-like bun. The optional lomito completo was a little much with chunks of avocado and a topping of ketchup, mustard, relish, sliced tomato, sauerkraut, pickled green chili pepper, and a slurry of mayonnaise.

On these long trips I do not follow any routine of exercising or a special eating schedules. There are days when I walk twenty miles and that gives me plenty of exercise. I don't regulate what I eat either, I just eat when I want and what I want to. I try to eat a balance that includes vegetables but they are hard to get at times when you are on the road. Fruit is plentiful in South America so I substituted fruits for the vegetables I normally eat. In the temperate zones of South America these fruits were apples, pears, peaches, melons and oranges. I don't take supplements but I do keep nutrition in mind.

I have eaten everything you can image and so far with no ill effect. When my brains says I am hungry, I eat. I don't think about food until a smell triggers the feeling. At 190 pounds and six-foot-one, a weight I have held for most of my life, I don't worry about food too much. I have worn the same size cloths since high school.

Having no fridge on the road keeps me slim. When I get home to Missouri I might pack on a few pounds because I spend more time sitting at the computer and going to the refrigerator to snack. Back home I only exercise when I am gardening or in my greenhouse.

I do eat when I am waiting though, like when waiting for a bus. I waited for many buses on this trip and in the stations I ate potato chips, pastry, and hot dogs with my coffee.

Bahia Valpariso

I had a good trip out of Santiago and arrived at Valparaiso, a port on the Pacific Coast. Bahia Valparaiso is divided by steep cliffs with two levels. You go between the two levels on Los Ascensors, elevators that have been in place since the 1800s. It rained the whole time I was there.

The reason for my side trip was to look for a freighter or any ship making the crossing to Easter Island. The freighters I found wouldn't haul passengers but the lady who ran the hostel where I stayed told me that the Chilean Navy runs ships occasionally to Easter Island in the course of administering the island. She told me that on these trips they take a few passengers.

I visited the Navy headquarters where an officer took me to the port where they offered me a three-week trip. I could board in two weeks and go to Easter Island. They did not intend to charge for the passage as near as I could determine.

While that was indeed a great opportunity, I wanted to reach Patagonia's parks before the December crowds. This navy trip would take too much time and I regretfully had to pass on the free trip to Easter Island.

I visited the Archaeological museum full of pre-Columbian artifacts from the Americas. While touring the museum I couldn't get Easter Island out of my mind. I had given up on boat passage so I decided to hunt for plane transport.

I left the museum and toured downtown Santiago, stopping in a travel agency to ask about transportation to Easter Island. They told me that to get a good price on plane fare I needed to book a week in advance. I moved on, keeping this option in mind for when I returned north.

I booked a half-day train ride to Chillan and traveled through the wine country from Santiago going south. Chile is a lush place where the Andes Mountains drain into the ocean while bringing plentiful pure water to every valley. The fields everywhere were full of orange colored wild flowers and where the flowers had established there were masses of brilliant orange.

Monkey Puzzle Tree

I spent the night in Chillian because I had been reading about an unusual tree called the Monkey Puzzle Tree. I booked a room in a private home where I had a private bath with a claw foot bathtub. I filled the tub with steaming water and soaked in luxury. Once cleaned and dressed, I headed out to the square of Chillan to see my first Monkey Puzzle Tree.

Chillan

On the way I saw great food markets. The lush farms of Chile enjoy a temperate spring climate which brings abundant fruits and vegetables to the cities. It was now early October and the early harvest of apricots was due soon. I walked streets lined with apricot trees, not quit ripe, and cherry trees full with sweet fruit. The private home where I lodged had a full orchard where I could sample ripe cherries picked from the tree.

During my tour of the city I found the Monkey Puzzle Tree. (Araucaria araucana) It seemed to have no relation to a monkey but did have some unusual characteristics including needles of triangular shape as stiff and sharp as a knife. Having more in common with an umbrella then a monkey, the national tree of Chile it turns out, grows plentiful in the south. From that point on to the south I saw many groves. Nobody, however, could tell me why the evergreen conifer with an edible seed is called the Monkey Puzzle Tree.

Cruising The Archipelago

I Packed my gear and left Chillan to continue south. I took a bus to Puerto Montt which lies on a huge bay at the northern end of the Archipelago de Los Chonos, an extensive area of Islands that run the length of Chile with the Pacific on one side and the Andes Mountains on the other. Coming down the road to Puerto Montt, I could see two sharply peaked volcanoes with a cap of snow on each one.

At Puerto Montt I looked for a ship going south to Puerto Natales. I finally found a suitable ship with Navimag and I booked a $400 USD, three-day cruise.

In the middle of October the ice clears out of the channels and the ships, combination passenger and cargo ferry, start their regular runs. The ship that I booked would enter the open sea for a short stretch and then weave in and out of the islands and channels of the archipelago. All through the voyage I could see to my left, the Andean mountains along the coast of Chile.

On board were trucks carrying cows, flatbed trucks loaded with heavy equipment lashed down by steel chains, supply trucks bound for the remote outposts along the way, and semis packed with consumer goods going south to the isolated towns of Tierra Del Fuego. We even hauled a semi-trailer that served as a traveling hotel.

The rolling hotel starts in the south where people get aboard at the southern terminus of the road. They then have a sightseeing trip through the Andes while heading north atop the cordillera. At night they sleep aboard their traveling hotel.

On our ship, above the vehicle deck, there were dorms and private rooms for passengers, dining rooms, and recreation rooms. We could go up to the bridge and watch the sailors work the ship and we could listen to the radio traffic while we watched the radar screen. They also allowed us to tour the engine room were several huge diesels propelled the ship day and night.

On the whole trip down, on the east side of the ship, we could see on the distant peaks of the Andes a cap of glaciers that jutted over the top and hung suspended. These caps of snow and ice are called hanging glaciers. At times they grow too big and they lean so far out that they break off. On occasion we could see this happen as the ice calved off the top of the mountain and streamed into the valley below like a waterfall of crystal ice. From the ship we could not hear the roar of the ice falling, but later, while hiking in the Andes, I did hear the calving, a thunderous explosion that boomed through the valleys and gave me a good scare.

The Chilean boat crew was a friendly bunch who could sure handle the passage. At times they maneuvered the vessel just twenty feet from shore where mountainous cliffs emerged from the water to soar steeply.

On occasion we saw orcas and porpoise rise from the slick surface and spurt water as they breathed. Always someone in the fifty or so passengers was at the rail on the lookout for Orcas. On spotting one they gave a shout, "Orca on the port side."
Quickly a dozen people ran to the rail to see the spouting and diving.

South Africans, Australians, Dutch, and of course the ubiquitous British traveler made up the passengers, a mix of the world's seasoned travelers, most on their way to camp out in the parks of Patagonia.

And among them a Missouri backpacker on his way to fulfill a lifetime dream: to pitch his tent at the bottom of the world.

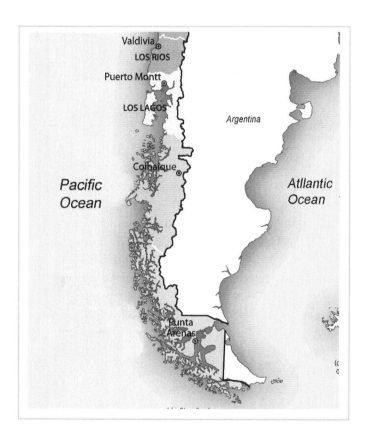

"Do not go where the path may lead, go instead where there is no path and leave a trail."   **Ralph Waldo Emerson**

9. Torres del Paine National Park

The boat crew did all they could to make the three-night cruise a pleasant trip. They served good meals three times a day and at night the activities director put on parties where the red and white Chilean wines flowed freely. They also ran movies of how one should go about camping, hiking, and staying alive in the parks of Patagonia.

In the afternoon we arrived in Puerto Natales, the Chilean part of Patagonia, located on the edge of what they call El Pampa. Tall peaks surrounded us as we pulled into the small port. This area has few roads; the boats become the link to civilization to the north.

Once the boat docked we had our choice of getting off or staying aboard until the next morning. Most of the passengers left the boat in the morning as did I, and we headed into town as the sun rose.

By now I had hooked up with two other hikers and we walked through the town of single story buildings to make our arrangements for camping in the park. In the small town we found Hospedaje Magdalena, a hostel with a great big pot bellied stove as the only heat; nights would be cold at that time of the year in Puerto Natales.

The air was fresh and crisp, blowing from the mountains, and the land glowed in the brittle sunlight. We had reached the southern extremes and we had frost on the grass each morning creating golden prisms that gleamed in the sunrise.

The town had a glorious fresh feeling to it as we walked while looking for a restaurant to have breakfast. My hiking companions were fit and seasoned hikers. The young man from South Africa was fair skinned, tall, and slender. He had hiked many of Africa's mountains. The young woman was in her thirties, an avid hiker from Sao Paulo Brazil. Both spoke English

After breakfast we went to a tourist office to book a camp in Torres del Paine National Park. The Park authorities carefully regulate camping and you must make reservations for your campsite or cabin. You reserve both food and lodging because in the high season the cabins and tent sites can fill up.

We paid for our meals and lodging in advance and that let them know how much food to cook and how full their cabins would be. In high season of December, January, and February, the park officials limit the number of visitors.

We booked the accommodations for our nights in the mountains and the next day a van came and picked us up at our hotels. We headed towards the park and went through customs with minimal formality at the border of Argentina. We then continued the three-hour drive to the park entrance were we paid the equivalent of $70 USD each to enter the park.

The driver then took us into the park for twenty miles to the staging point where he dropped us off. From there we were on our own for five days in Torre del Paines National Park, no guides, no rangers, and not many rules; we were free to hike safely or free to hike foolishly and die, it was our choice.

Patagonia Hikes

The van had dropped us at a staging area where there was a campsite but we agreed to hike towards our reserved cabin for our first nights lodging. We weren't sure just how far the cabin was but we struck out anyway for our camp and luckily after seven hours of hard hiking we made the cabin with two hours of light to spare.

Two more hikers that we knew from the boat trip had joined us and we had five in our group by this time, the South African man, the Brazilian woman, a German woman, and an American woman in her sixties. We had all socialized on the boat trip and since we all spoke English and got on well we

91

decided that we would book the trip together although, while we hiked, we each went at our own pace. That pace usually saw the young African man way out in front, me and the 30-year old Brazilian woman a few miles behind, and the German woman in her twenties and the American woman in her sixties, trailing far behind. This allowed us each to enjoy the scenery at our own pace and to try the many side trails if we chose.

We planned to meet each night at our pre-booked camp but we would all arrive at different times throughout the day.

On our first morning, I left camp before dawn in a light overcast to climb into the mountains. I reached the base of the mountain and then climbed hand over hand up a steep bank strewn with big boulders. A snow squall came in and I continued hiking through a light snowfall. Snow continued to fall while I hiked for half a day, climbing towards a clearing were I could get a view of the basin, a glacial cirque surrounded on three sides by steep peaks. When I finally got to the plateau, the snow was so thick I could not see. I sat and waited for two hours but the snow never let up. I never did have my view on that hike; I reluctantly had to climb back down without ever having my view of the valley. I reached the cabin well before dark.

Each night the cabins provided bunks where we spread our own sleeping bags. We each brought some food and we were able to find water everywhere, either glacial streams that are melting faster then they have in recent history or in storage jugs at the cabins.

I brought dried fruits and nuts in my pack for evening meals and bought breakfast at each cabin were a park staff member cooked in a kitchen of sorts. Breakfast each day cost twenty USD.

When you consider that the staff packs in all the food by horseback and you are miles from civilization in the most exquisite scenery of glacial lakes, meadows of wildflowers, ancient trees struggling to grow, and steep-sided mountains with snow-capped peaks, breakfast at $20 USD was fairly priced.

"God look at those mountains," I would exclaim to no one in particular in a moment of awe during a hike. Those peaks provided many moments of awe. I couldn't believe how steep they were. Everywhere you looked, streams carried water that had been locked in ice for thousands of years and was now racing through the valleys and cascading towards the ocean. In this remarkable setting, I considered a twenty-dollar breakfast of eggs, bacon, coffee, and yogurt a bargain.

The cabins are spaced so that a hiker can spend eight to ten hours going between stops. I hiked eight hours each day over trails, at times flooded with water, where park employees had built walkways and at some places, suspension bridges across low areas. The trails were well marked in the 240,000-hectare park but you could get in trouble if you were not careful. In the high season of December, January, and February, however, there would be many hikers to give assistance.

I saw herds of guanaco, a small llama, while hiking but saw no dangerous animals. None live in the park as far as I know but some hikers believed the park was home to mountain lion.

The trails were well maintained but took some caution. On one trail I walked a knife-edge as I looked down a thousand feet into the abyss of valleys on both sides where streams were running. On misstep on that trail could have been my last.

Glacial Lakes

On the second day we headed to the next cabin, a long hike to a camp just below a huge rock wall. The park's many sheer cliffs attract world-class climbers and we passed their camps where private huts are reserved for those that visit to scale rock faces. We spent the next two days hiking along the base of a group of mountains and on the forth day we came into a beautiful glacial lake surrounded by peaks. The park has many glacial lakes of various sizes, most are blue with minerals suspended in the ice. The blue is so intense that it looks like dye but the color is a natural occurrence.

On the way to the lake we came to a suspension bridge with a crossroads trail and a trail that led up the mountain. I split from the group and took the high trail where I climbed to the base of the peaks. As I walked around the cliffs I could see hanging glaciers high above. Suddenly, with a roar like thunder, the hanging glacier broke from the high ridge and sent ice crashing down in a crystal waterfall that cascaded over the face of the cliff and into the valley. The ice slammed to the ground at the base of the mountain with a deafening roar.

A little more cautious now, I continued walking the base of the mountain. Soon I came to a plateau where the wind was so intense I could barely stand. I had to sit down and prop myself against a rock or hook my arm around a gnarly tree to make photographs. Within a few miles I had passed through several microclimates of extremes as I hiked.

I had incredible views in every direction as shadows grew longer and my stamina ebbed. I had been through enough of natures extremes, fatigued but elated I hiked back down to the swinging bridge and then towards the lodge.

We had booked rooms at the lodge before the trip, anticipating the need by this time for hot water bathing and cooked food. And what a treat, for the first time in almost a week we had hot showers. I stood for an eternity in the shower washing away week of pain and Patagonian dirt.

After cleaning up, we met at the bar and went to the restaurant where the staff served us a free drink and brought us a dinner of soup salad and a main course which we savored after our days of dried foods on the trail.

That evening the trip ended for the German and the American woman but the African man, the Brazilian woman, and I stayed on to hike the next day. We headed out at dawn for a seven-hour walk to a glacier were there was a cabin in which we could spend the night.

On this hike I took a fall, the first one for me. I was coming down a steep trail when I stepped on a loose boulder and went head over heels down the path. Miraculously I had no injuries. I was hiking with an American man at this point, the Brazilian woman and South African man had gone on ahead. After checking for broken bones, I found that I was still whole and I resumed the hike without much more than a few new aches and pains.

It was raining most of the day but we saw some scenery that included waterfalls. We then reached the glacial lake where the cabin was located. We stashed our packs in the hut at the edge of the lake and continued hiking up to the glacier. We hiked the trail without seeing much but suddenly we rounded a corner of some rocks and there it was; Grey Glacier. We stopped and stood in awe. What a feeling to be so close to a glacier as it calved and shed blue ice into the lake.

I was struck by the power of nature. A new feeling came over me coming from my feet up through my body, a feeling hard to describe. I can only remember a few times in life being awed like that: standing in front Michelangelo's David, standing at the Devils Throat waterfall, and now, in my sixth decade of life, standing in front of a huge glacier in Patagonia and watching as it shed sheets of blue ice that had been formed in prehistoric times.

You are never too old to be awed by the power and beauty of nature in this world and I looked forward to many more days of awe. Little did I know that soon I would stand in front of an even larger glacier in Park Nacional Los Glaciares in Argentina. Moreno Glacier would top them all but before that I would have a date with the penguins.

"Clay lies still, but blood is a rover.   Breaths aware that will not keep.
Up, lad, when the journey is over there'll be time enough to sleep."
A. E. Housman

10. Punta Arenas

It was at this time, standing beside Grey Glacier, that my Nikormat film camera stopped working. I managed to run off two or three frames and then the film would not advance. Here I experienced a lifetime high one second and a profound low the next; but that is life. I will always have an image in my mind of that blue ice tumbling into the water from the side of the glacier.

I met the other hikers at the cabin on the lake and we spent the night. In the morning we hiked back to Refugio Pehoe, a new lodge where we indulged ourselves again with showers and then a meal in the dining room. We stayed one night and in the morning we went by boat over the glacial lake, Lago Pehoe.

As the boat crossed the lake, a grand view of the peaks beneath which we had hiked came into view in bright sunlight. I had no camera to give a last goodbye shot to this fantastic park where I had hiked for the past five days but I had memories that will last forever.

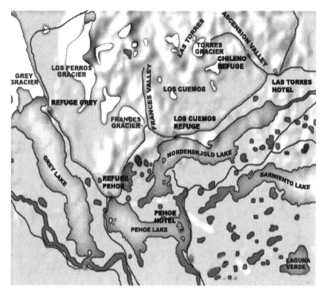

The boat dropped us at the bus staging area and from there we went back to Puerto Natales where I said farewell to my hiking companions.

From Puerto Natales I caught a bus that took half a day to reach Punta Arenas. I walked from the bus station in Punta Arenas to look for lodging. On the way I met a woman who offered a place to stay in her home, a common occurrence in this remote area where the women try to make a little extra money to support the household. I stayed two nights in this interesting town.

Punta Arenas had once been an oil town, a port for ships transiting the straits of Magellan, and a center for wool production, a wealthy one at that. The interesting buildings in town were houses once owned by the wealthy that had been converted to museums to the various industries. Many upscale tour boats leave for first class trips around the islands of Tierra del Fuego to bring Punta Arenas tourist revenue as a staging area for trips to the national parks.

I bought stocking caps in Punta Arenas. These wool caps were constructed with a soft flannel lining that stops the chilly winds better than any hat I have ever owned. After trying one on I realized how warm they were and how often I misplace things; I bought three. I was determined at this point to continue heading south as far as I could go so I knew that these hats could be useful.

I wanted a nice meal before I hit the road again so I went to La Luna Restaurant, a bright blue and yellow place full of Latin rhythms. I ordered a Pisco Sour with a meal of steak and potatoes, the first steak I had in this land of great Argentinean beef.

Ushuaia

Next I boarded a bus to Rio Gallegos and although it is north and I wanted to go south, I was forced to go north because there are no roads south from Punta Arenas. I switched buses in Rio Gallegos and then headed south to cross the Straits of Magellan by ferry. The road, Route 190, the Pan American Highway, the road where I had first traveled by bus in Mexico, ended in Ushuaia,

Argentina, the most southerly town in South America. Here I had planned to end my southerly journey.

When I arrived in Ushuaia, however, I realized that six ships were taking passengers to Antarctica and I found myself wanting to go along. I suddenly had the urge to plant my hikers on the southern most point in the world.

Two days of research told me that I would need some equipment and supplies. Antarctica was the topic on every travelers lips on main street in Ushuaia where dozens of shops catered to tourists heading for Antarctica. Early December starts the season and although it is the start of their summer, it was still cool and you needed winter garb.

I would need rubber boots, sunglasses, parka, and I reasoned, wine, cheese, and crackers. The local buzz was all about Antarctica and the word was stock up, so I shopped for some items in town.

I bought rubber boots thinking that I would never find my size thirteens but was surprised when I did. By the middle of the second day I had collected the needed equipment and was committed to going to Antarctica. I went to the tour office and booked the three thousand dollar ticket. I then waited three days for the ship.

Later I found that the ship provided everything for a nominal price including rental of parkas and boots and all the snacks we needed.

In Ushuaia, while waiting, I dined in style at Parrilla restaurants. They featured grilled meats, roasted lamb on a skewer, Argentina style, and chicken, beef, and sausage. Lots of other activities keep the tourists busy including horseback riding, trekking, bicycle riding, skiing, and boat trips to islands. Some of the Islands in the area were occupied by flocks of roosting penguins and others were home to herds of seals.

I knew at that time that I was at the end of the earth; the sun would no sooner set then it would suddenly rise again.

Cape Horn Aboard

The day came to board the ship and we met in a hotel staging area where we handed in our luggage which went on ahead to our ship cabins. We went by bus to the docks and right to the ship boarding area where we picked up our key and deposited our passport for an inspection by Argentine officials.

Underway by mid morning, we headed out of the beagle channel and past Cape Horn. During that night we entered the roughest seas in the world, the Drake Passage. We were on our way to Antarctica.

Huge swells rocked the ship for most of the night and through the next day. The erratic motion of the turbulent sea rendered me beyond queasy.

Finally in the mid day, we entered still waters; the waves calmed and so did my stomach. We still had no land in sight as we left the passage, just Albatross and flocks of sea birds that trailed the ship.

Antarctica
We were four days on the ocean passage, two days each way and then nine days in Antarctica on the thirteen-day trip. All this time, the passengers had total access to the ships engine room, bridge, and kitchen. Tours were available most any time. The Captain gave us comfort; he was a Nordic sailor familiar with cold weather sailing and icebergs.

Each passenger had an invitation to the Captain's table for dinner and free cocktails. These diners included a speech by the captain and a crewmember. During this speech they made it clear that we needed to be careful during the voyage, falling overboard for instance would be fatal. We were not to harass the animals on shore, we were warned, and we must be particularly cautious with the penguins. They were unafraid of humans and their bite could be serious enough to require stitches.

Once we reached the continent and we saw our first masses of ice, the crew posted schedules of the shore visits which included several trips ashore each day.

Each morning I rose before seven for coffee and then they served a great breakfast of eggs and ham, cheese, coffee, and tea.

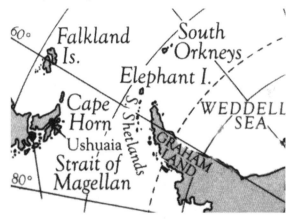

After breakfast we suited up and loaded an inflatable to go ashore. Usually we landed on shelf ice but occasionally we could see rocks. On most trips ashore, however, we saw nothing but ice and flocks of penguins.

The penguins were fun to watch as they came leaping out of the water to waddle over the ice. Often we saw seals in groups up on the ice. All the while, orcas cruised offshore in their hunt for an easy penguin or seal dinner.

We had to be cautious because strong winds could come on-shore unexpectedly and they would force you to your knees to avoid being blown over. When this happened and we were near the shore there was danger that the wind would tumble us into the frozen sea.

We had a system of numbered tags that we removed from a board when we went ashore so that the crew knew when each passenger was back on the ship.

The crew served us lunch at noon and this included wine and cocktails to accompany the gourmet meals served with fresh rolls and fresh-baked bread. The menu at times included exotics like llama and Emu served along with beef and shrimp, soup and salad, vegetable and dessert of cakes and puddings.

We were aboard the ship Antarctic Dream, with a crew who used every opportunity to entertain us.

The crew included an ornithologist, a biologist, and an expert in natural history. These guides presented photos and dissertations each night at the recreation room.

Several countries maintain stations in Antarctica to conduct research. One such station was researching the thawing of the ice. We visited several of the research stations on shore where we took place in guided tours.

Each day we passed icebergs as we went further south until one day we went as far south as the ship could go and we actually broke ice as we went. There were magic vistas of glaciers looming out of the mist as we entered sheltered bays where we boarded the inflatable and slipped through the chunks of ice to reach the shore.

Penguins

At several of our shore visits the penguins crowded the shoreline to make their nest of whatever rocks they could find. A shortage of rocks caused many a squabble among the birds as they went at each other with thrashing wings. They fought continually over the scarce nesting material but they did no apparent damage to each other.

In this surreal deepfreeze the only thing alive were the birds, fish, penguins, seals and the algae that grows on the rocks.

Every night the naturalists presented a movie about what we would do the following day and briefed us on the life we might see. These presentations even included some Shakleton lore. Bright clear air in the evening and mornings brought the most unusual light that I have ever seen. During the visit, huge glaciers calved and made their presence known with rumbles that echoed throughout the sea of icebergs.

One afternoon we pulled into a bay close to shore and circled the bay as glaciers fell on all sides. We had an outdoor barbecue on deck where the crew grilled chicken and sausage as we drank wine and watched the amazing calving of glaciers all around us.

At sunrise one morning we went into a bay full of icebergs and climbed on top of some of them. A few of us had a snowball fight while on an iceberg of unusual colors caused by the continual slapping of waves. Later we visited an English research station where we found a whale skeleton up on the ice.

One of the rules that the crew insisted on was that we never leave anything onshore. It seemed that cigarette smokers never got the word on this one, however; they just stubbed their butts out on the ice.

On another trip ashore we entered a volcanic lagoon were the water was so warm that we were able to swim. A few of us put on trunks and actually swam in the Antarctic Ocean from a black volcanic sand beach.

Lots of warm drink followed that trip. The crew had Courvoisier and hot coffee waiting to warm us up when we returned to the ship.

On another trip ashore I had basalt rocks with surreal rock formations on one side of me while on the other side, seals and penguins moved over the ice. I felt like I had entered a Dali painting.

Each day of the tour through Antarctica we went ashore in the morning and then again in the afternoon. We stepped on the continent of Antarctica at least fourteen times and at the last visit, the crew awarded us a certificate stating as much. I marveled that I had reached the bottom of the world and I felt privileged to be there.

I know that these trips might someday be halted because of the damage that so many tourists are causing. I have read rumors about the end of tours to this area. I felt lucky to have made the trip and to be one of the privileged few on earth to sail through the Drake Passage and to circle Cape Horn. The last night on board, we had a party and the wine and liquor flowed freely.

To circle Cape Horn earns a sailor the right to put a ring in his ear but I will pass on that one.

Moreno Glacier

After the Antarctic cruise I returned to Ushuaia and then bussed back towards the border with Chile to El Calafate. From this tourist town full of shops that cater to the visitors to Moreno Glacier, I booked a tour. A bus came by the hotel next morning and we headed for the glacier.

On the way through a prairie surrounded by mountains we passed Gauchos in their felt hats and high boots as they tended cattle in the high plains of Argentina.

We reached the Perito Moreno Glacier and visited several viewing places were we could see the glacier calve. This glacier, we learned, is one of the few glaciers that are growing rather then receding. No one knows why.

We took a boat tour to the face of the glacier to get a closer view. That feeling of awe came over me again, awe at the sublime power of nature to render such colors and shapes. The calving demonstrated the ability of nature to self-renew while always creating unique shapes and texture. We all just stood in quiet reverence before the power of nature.

When I left El Calafate I headed for El Chalten and to the Fitzroy Range, a destination lure for world-class climbers and ardent hikers. Passing beside the Rio Fitzroy in the valley I could see the Fitzroy Range, a dramatic sight because of the steepness of the peaks.

El Chalten, a frontier town at the foot of the Fitzroy range is rustic, so the stories went, and you must bring the appropriate Argentine peso because there would be no ATM or money changer.

I headed for the free campground outside of town to pitch my tent in a site where I could get water and had access to a bathroom. After securing everything I walked back into town for a dinner of chicken and potatoes.

Turns out that the town does have an ATM but still was not much more than a hikers base and tour station.

I toured the town looking for local information about camping in the Fitzroy Range. I bought six days worth of supplies in town including a bottle of wine. Lunchmeat and bread, which I would eat early on, granola bars, dried fruit, and nuts.

On this trip into the mountains, I planned to do some strenuous hiking so I traveled light. I did not lug a stove and I did not miss my coffee. I had all I needed.

What I have is all I have and If I don't have it I don't need it. I saw many campers that brought the whole house with them and I felt lucky that I can live without anything but air and water for a short time.

I hiked for five days in the Fitzroys. A couple of times I got lost but the well-marked trails always got me back on familiar track. A couple of climbs took all I had but the scenery was worth the effort. The campsites are well marked while the camping is restricted to the established camps where there are latrine facilities.

Each night I camped at a different spot near water. No fires are allowed except in stoves. I saw few campers as it was early in the season and cold at night but my 32-degree square-shaped single bag kept me warm.

On the sixth day I returned to El Chalten to set my tent up and then I headed to town for a good meal: a hearty Argentinean stew made with vegetables and meat with homemade bread.

On the restaurant wall I saw a poster with a striking photo of the heads at Easter Island. I felt my feet move and the unmistakably familiar pang that usually precedes my next trip. Could Easter Island still fit in my plans?

"Too often. . . I would hear men boast of the miles covered that day, rarely of what they had seen." Louis L'Amour

11. Easter Island

From El Chalten I headed north on a local bus with the intent to later hook up with a series of buses that went over the Carreterra Austral highway. This is a scenic road that runs right beside the Andean peaks. Sounds ideal but the road is in harsh country and is in varying states of repair.

This route did offer beautiful scenery with high lakes surrounded by mountains but the road in places was barely passable after the harsh winter. We passed tiny villages along this route that were just emerging from their winter slumber. They bloomed with springtime flowers and flowering fruit trees. Lupines crowded the roadsides while cherry trees and apricot groves grew in the fields beyond.

Many rivers came streaming from the mountains, feeding these lush valleys as the winter snows melted. Guanaco, llama, and Emus grazed in the wild, far out in the fields and meadows below the snow-capped mountains.

I kept working north through this idyllic scene on a 600 mile network of dirt roads, gravel tracks, and finally pavement as I headed for Puerto Aisen where I would catch a Navmag cruise ship north through the archipelago and back to my starting place at Puerto Montt.

When the boat tied up in Puerto Montt I didn't get too far from the dock before a lady approached with an offer of a room in her home and I took it. I wanted to stay two nights to rest and didn't have the energy to shop for a place.

Rested after a good nights sleep, I toured the area by local bus, making a day trip north 13 miles to Puerto Varas. Out of Puerto Varas, a quaint town on Todos los Santos Lake, I took another bus through a beautiful valley to the foot of Calbucao and Osorno Volcanoes at the village of Petrohue. From the village I hiked along the river and then up to the Osornos Volcano for a memorable view of the river valley between the two volcanoes. I returned to Puerto Montt in late afternoon, my memory full again of images of natural beauty. I rose early the next day to catch a bus to Santiago, a 28-hour trip.

Easter Island

After arriving in Santiago I took the metro to the house where I had first stayed on my way south. The lady had a full house but had another place where she offered me a private room on a tree-lined street for the same price.

I had earlier made a reservation via the internet for a trip by the airline, Lan Chile, to Easter Island. Once I arrived in Santiago I confirmed my reservation and they booked me on the following day for a $700 round trip flight, a figure about twice what a Chilean pays.

The airline flies three times a week to Easter Island, 2,500-miles off the Chilean coast. Locally called Rapa Nui by its 2,500 residents, 70% of whom are native Pascuenses, speakers of a Polynesian language. Easter Island officially speaks Spanish.

Our jet touched down at Hanga Roa airfield and from there I walked the entire island the first day, about 12 hours of hiking. The path took me through all the heads, including some that had been knocked down by a huge wave and had been replanted with the help of donations from the Japanese.

Volcanic rock was everywhere and although the Island had been denuded of trees long ago, there now are Eucalyptus trees growing.

Most heads faced inland with just a few facing the sea, one of the many enigmas that still defy understanding by researchers who try to make some sense of the Island archaeologically.

The stones tell researchers that the inhabitants started carving the colossal figures in the 7th century AD and continued up until the 15th Century. The rest is a mystery

I stayed in a private home out on the tip of the island at the edge of the ocean where I paid $35 a night. I stayed four nights, plenty of time to see the whole island, including the volcano, the standing heads, and the quarry where the ancient people carved the heads.

I was hitchhiking one day when a local gal picked me up. I asked about all the horses that I saw roaming free.

"Oh yes," she said, in a matter of fact way, "We eat them"

Midnight Tango

I flew back to Santiago and hopped right on a local bus to the first class bus terminal where I got an overnight ticket 950 miles due east to Buenos Aires. When I arrived in Buenos Aires I walked around the terminal to the Metro, locally called the Subte, to head to the San Telmo area, the region where the Argentine Tango originated.

My hostel was within a block of the metro station. Nearby on the corner of Defensa and

Humberto the Plaza Dorrego becomes an outdoor nightclub on weekends were Tango is serious entertainment.

The clubs get rolling at around midnight and the party goes until dawn for the Portenos, as the people of Buenos Aires call themselves. Tables crowd the whole square and the center becomes a dance floor as couples demonstrate the Argentine Tango in all its nuances. They then invite everybody to dance the tango.

I love to watch the dance and was encouraged to try myself a few times, inviting a lady who was standing nearby. We both laughed as we went through the motions and tried a few dances in a vain attempt to master the complicated steps. We then sat back down and had a drink and enjoyed the show.

I have danced all my life but the tango is difficult to learn, especially when it includes several regional versions. Without my felt hat and suspenders I just couldn't let my inner dancer free.

I spent five days in the hostel and toured the city and included the Plaza de Mayo where Juan Peron and Eva often stood to address the people. The grieving women of Buenos Aires, The Madre de la Plaza de Mayo, still march through the city on Thursday in front of the notorious Pink Palace. They still demand to know where their loved ones had gone during the, "Dirty War."

Buenos Aires hugs the bank of the Rio de la Plata at the eastern edge of the Atlantic Ocean and on the border of Uruguay. I headed into Uruguay via a ferry to Colonia, crossing the huge river estuary thirty miles across. I should have bought my ticket earlier because the ticket agency was a mad house of people clamoring for tickets but I finally boarded for the three-hour trip.

Colonia del Sacramento is a small town on the river's Uruguay side and a quaint and beautiful colonial town at that. I went over there to see this town after reading about it. I booked onto the Hotel Colonial.

Walk Of The Hawk

There at Colonia I met an 80-year old guy who was in his 15th year of walking around the world. His name was Harry McGinnis and he was doing his walk in sections of many months of travel after which he would return home to Texas.

The conditioning of this guy impressed me. He had a full head of gray hair and a splendid physique for any guy over forty. He was able to carry an 80-pound pack while also lugging a ten-pound staff as a protective weapon that he claimed to have used more than a few times. For an eighty-year old he was remarkable: spry and as robust as a man half his age.

"Walk of the Hawk" he called himself and he was an inspiration to travelers. And of course, he tells it all on his website.

New Years Tango

From Colonia I caught a bus to Montevideo the next morning. I wanted to visit the capital of Uruguay and I also needed a visa for my return to Brazil as I headed north.

The Brazilian immigration official, however, just wasn't too friendly and she insisted that I needed a return transportation ticket to get the visa. Usually I am able to talk my way around this and make the official understand that I am passing through and I am able to get the visa without having a return ticket. The officials do this because they want to be sure that you have a way out of their country. At the border crossing, however, no inspector ever asks to see your return ticket.

The Brazilian official in this instance did not relent as we talked, so I decided to go north without passing through Brazil. I returned to Buenos Aires, via Colonia, where I spent Christmas.

When I reached Buenos Aires I booked into a different hostel closer to the tango action at the Plaza Dorrego. A considerable upgrade it turned out, Hostel San Telmo offered a free breakfast and much more comfort.

On December 27, I went out to the Recoleta cemetery to see the burial place of the Perons. I continued my tour of the city museums and sights including downtown which has great shopping areas with pedestrian-only streets and upscale shops. Many of the buildings reminded me of French European architecture.

At other times I went to San Telmo and just sat on a bench and ate white chocolate ice cream while watching the people go by.

I had a surprise one day when I met the German man who I traveled with in Panama on the sailboat through the San Blas Islands. It really didn't amaze me to run into him again, I know that more than likely I will run into the same people several times on a long trip. We all travel the same trail: the backpackers trail around the world. All the sights are on the same trails, we all head to the same places. I have run into the same people four or five times in different countries on long trips.

I also reacquainted with a couple that I met on my first stay in Buenos Aires, a Dutch couple who were traveling around the world by air. I joined them for New Years champagne and tango dancing on the Plaza Dorrego where we met another traveler from Australia. We sat in the square and watched tango dancing while we drank red Malbecs and Champagnes at the old bars with their open windows. We then danced to the music while doing our best Argentine tango.

We partied for what felt like long into the morning but when we left Plaza Dorrego for our hotels, the local people were just starting to get warmed up.

I toasted the New Year and said my farewells to Buenos Aires. I looked forward to the last leg of my journey, a bus north on the second of January heading to a town called Villazon where I planned to start my trip home.

I was feeling elated at the dawn of a new year and the end of an exciting trip. Every bus ride and boat ride had been flawless, every person that I met, happy and friendly, how could I know what a downer I was in for next.

"The open road is a beckoning, a strangeness, a place where a man can lose himself." **William Least Heat Moon**

12. Bolivia And Home

Bad Bus Ride

I was on my way north, on my way home with a bus ticket to the border town of Villazon in Bolivia. The bus stopped, however, before we reached the border, a demonstration was blocking the road.

We could move no further and we had to leave the bus. I started walking towards the border not knowing how far it was but when I asked a few passengers and then saw that all the passengers were leaving the bus and heading for the border I knew it couldn't be too far. After five miles we reached Villazon and crossed into Bolivia.

Next I had the most difficult bus ride of my entire eight months of travel. Although I was only a day and a half on the road, it was the worst day and a half of my trip.

I passed through customs and walked to the bus station where I bought a ticket. I then realized that the clerk had given me the wrong ticket. After a tussle I got the right ticket and just as I did I heard the call for the bus to Oruro, my destination.

By the time I reached the bus there was one seat available at the back and it proved to be the worst seat on the bus. On the all night ride, I bounced up and down with my head hitting the ceiling of the bus. When the bus came down, I came slamming down with it and my body smacked down on the hard torn seats where springs stuck out and the stuffing was pounded flat.

We stopped at places along the way for bathroom breaks as we crossed the Southern Alto Plano and these stops were interesting. The passengers left the bus and took to the nearest fence or wall, tree or building, to squat or stand and pee. Ladies squatted next to men in the semi-darkness without embarrassment. The rest stops had absolutely no amenities, none that is except barbeque rotisseries where chicken and French fries were available.

Oruro

Finally after the most miserable ride of my life we arrived at Oruro at about seven in the morning. We were on the Alto Plano at a town that was once the capital of tin mining. Everything seemed to be colored dirt red in the old part of town, a complete city of ochre colored buildings.

There were 170,000 people still living in the once prosperous town, which included a large native Indian population who managed to scrape a bleak living from farming and the little mining that was left in the mountains.

Carnival was the one highlight left to Oruro. The pre-lent cultural festival is noted throughout the world for its costumes and folk traditions. The town also still serves as a transportation hub for busses throughout Bolivia and provided my bus transit to the next station.

I had time to kill before the next bus so I went into a restaurant near the station to have some breakfast. I sat but the waitress behind the counter paid no attention to me. I sat for a long while and they would not serve me. The more I hollered for service the more the waitress avoided me. I went to another restaurant nearby and the same thing happened. It came to mind at this time how other races must feel when they suffer discrimination. They wouldn't serve me because I was white and different from them. This was a new experience for me and it proved the value of travel as a means to experience events that would otherwise never happen. Even when events are unpleasant they teach.

I finally went to the main plaza where a Spanish-speaking waitress served me and I did get my eggs, beans, rice, and tortillas for breakfast.

Oruro was a town used up by the mining operation as near as I could see. Bleak and backward, the town has run out its string and barely hangs on, now depending on the annual carnival to draw some tourists and serving as the only town on the only road north to Lake Titicaca.

From the high ground in the plaza of Oruro I could read the town's disturbing history. All around me I could see scarred land and gouged out mountains where mining companies had ripped the land apart and left it in a shambles once they removed the ore.

Persian Carpets

I bought a ticket for La Paz in Bolivia. The bus left at ten PM, reaching La Paz in mid morning. I had visited La Paz before so I knew where I wanted to stay. I headed towards the Hotel Torino in the middle of the large city.

I was on my way home at that point, back to Missouri, so I spent just two nights in La Paz.

La Paz is a city of over a million people, located at 3,500 meters above sea level on the Southern Alto Plano where the land drops severely. In a canyon at the edge of this extreme, the city of La Plaz occupies a valley on a tributary of the Amazon River. The position of La Paz puts it too high in the mountain valley for most airliners to fly into. Consequently it is an expensive place to buy airline tickets from the few airlines that do serve the airport. I was looking for air passage to Colombia but the price in La Paz was too much.

I spent the day relaxing in La Paz. While walking the streets in the wealthy section of town I spotted a store selling Persian carpets. I collect Persian carpets so I had to stop when I saw a sign advertising 50% off.

In I went and found that they were good quality Cashmere carpets, some of cotton and some of wool. I bought a nice Persian carpet that came from Kazan, a great center of carpet making in Iran. The rug sold for $150 so I bought it and bought another one made in Cashmere, a prayer carpet of cotton. Now I had some extra baggage that I would need to carry with me on my return and I needed to wrap them in opaque plastic.

Next day I bought my bus ticket to Copacabana, a small town on lake Titicaca at the border of Bolivia and Peru. This little town is not much more than a transport hub for trips to Peru. Of note, however, Isla del Sol, five miles offshore in Titicaca, was once the most important religious site in South America, the place, according to ancient legend, where the sun and the moon were created.

From Copacabana I caught a bus heading for Arequipa. With no roads or bridges across the lake, the bus made the lake passage aboard a raft. The passengers boarded a boat while the empty bus crossed the lake on a rickety raft. Later, on the opposite shore, bus, raft, and passenger met and were again on the road.

From there I was on my way north on the east side of Peru to Quito in Ecuador but first I wanted to make a side trip to Lima. An article in the airline magazine on the plane from Easter Island was still fresh in my mind. It described a store in Lima that sold baby alpaca scarves, a wool as fine as cashmere, and I wanted to take a look.

Baby Alpaca

While on my detour to lima to shop for these baby alpaca scarves, I stayed at the Hostel Espana.

I spent two days shopping and eventually bought five scarves of different colors. Eight feet long and of the finest wool you can get except for Vicuna, I couldn't resist them at $20 dollars each. I bought browns, grays, and blacks that I will use as gifts. From Lima I headed for Quito, a straight shot, where I spent one night and then I caught a bus early the next morning for Cali in Columbia. I had at that point been on the road for three days so I stayed in Cali while resting and looking for a flight to Panama.

On my second day in Cali, I booked a flight that took me to Bogata and then to Panama City. I had no intention of riding the sailboat back although I did enjoy the cruise through the Islands of San Blas. After eight months on the road I was ready to go home.

From Panama I sped through Central America again and my next rest stop was Zipolite Beach on the Pacific Coast of Oaxaca, Mexico, a place where I feel at home.

I reacquainted with friends at Zipolite and rested for two weeks, doing nothing much more than laying in a hammock, reading books, and recovering from eight months of travel.

Regardless of my exhaustion after months in South American, I sat in a hammock reading the Divinci Code and thinking about taking a trip to Europe to see the many churches mentioned in the book.

From Zipolite I took a van over Oaxaca's mountains to Oaxaca City where I caught a bus

back to Missouri, a nonstop 46-hour trip except for
several changes of buses.

Home

Dawn always seems to great me in Springfield
when I return form the road. A taxi picked me up at
the bus station and on the way to the ranch I
stopped in to the grocery store and picked up coffee,
spring water, and apples, my breakfast many
mornings.

Finally back home after eight months on the
road, I made coffee and sat on the porch eating
apples while looking out on the rolling hills.

My attention then went to the garden where soon
I would start planting cabbages, lettuce, spinach,
onions, garlic, and radishes. As I planned out each
row in my head, a thread of questions ran through
my mind; would I ever stay put long enough to
harvest what my seeds would bring.

Zipolite Beach, Pacific Coast Oaxaca

Stranded In Chicken
A Year On The Road in South and North America

By David Rice

Part II
Freedom To Be Peculiar

*"For West is where we all plan to go
some day.
It is where you go when the land gives
out and the old-field pines encroach.
It is where you go when you get the
letter saying: Flee, all is discovered.
It is where you go when you look down
at the blade in your hand and the blood
on it.
It is where you go when you are told
that you are a bubble on the tide of
empire.
It is where you go when you hear that
thar's gold in them-thar hills.
It is where you go to grow up with the
country.
It is where you go to spend your old
age.
Or it is just where you go."*

Robert Penn Warren

*"The real voyage of discovery consists not in seeking new landscapes,
but in having new eyes."   Marcel Proust*

13. Freedom To Be Peculiar

I rested a few days after my return from South
America and then I started work on my garden. As
usual my mind wandered to places far from the
Missouri Ozarks. I knew that this would happen; I
am a traveler deep in my heart; my feet like to be
moving over new turf; I just can't stay put.

It is always about new scenery, new experience,
new adventure, new food, and new music. I could
stay home and hang with the old townies anytime
but they are an unhappy bunch. They have tread the
same paths so often that they have made ruts. They

talk about people they once knew with a nasty edge and an envious attitude: past deeds, past conquests, and, very rarely, past failures. Usually they are the hero of each story but it is always in the past. I want to live in the present and future.

I liked the rush I got from a few dicey situations on my South America trip. The deserted beach, the hikes on the sides of Calbuco and Osomo Volcanos, The ship passage through the Drake Channel, the long bus rides to so many exotic places. Bus ride, boat ride, bike ride, or walk; I just like to travel.

I carved out rows for my seeds and laid down enough mulch to make it self-sustaining but I knew that I would never see the first sprouts. Soon enough, a letter came that would have me on the road again.

It was an invitation that got me; it was from a friend, a retired art teacher who lives in the Ozarks of Arkansas part of the year and in Seattle the remainder of the year where his son lives. He invited me to visit him in Seattle.

With not much more than onion, garlic, and carrot seeds in the ground, I gave in to the need to sooth my itchy feet; I made plans for a short visit to Seattle.

My friend went to Seattle years ago and found rents expensive so he bought an old distressed Chris Craft and restored it to pristine condition. He made a live-aboard of the 46-foot antique and now when he visits, he stays on the boat at a marina on Seattle's Lake Union.

After I finished planting my garden I took to the road again and was soon on my way to Seattle.

"Where are you going?" I asked myself a dozen times just before the trip as my backpack grew larger with tent gear, hikers, and cooking equipment. The traveler in me knew that, in the back of my mind somewhere, I had a plan brewing for travel beyond Seattle.

And sure enough when I left Missouri, I hefted a forty-pound pack with all my tenting gear as if I was going on another eight-month jaunt.

Freemont

I was soon in Seattle and on the boat in the middle of downtown Fremont. I was touring the lake beneath the Fremont Bridge with my friend in his mahogany Chris Craft.

Some days we joined a friend of his who restores boats for a living and we toured in his boat. We cruised east over to Portage Bay or west on the Lake Washington Ship Canal to Salmon Bay and the Chittenden locks where we could tie up and visit the fish ladder to watch the Salmon. Other days we just sat and watched the boats come through the locks. I stayed three weeks touring with these two guys as they recounted legends about Seattle, about a mysteriously derelict marijuana boat, about suicide bridge, the Freemont Troll, a naked parade, and about the Freemont motto, "Freedom to be Peculiar."

Suicide Bridge

Seattle is a quirky place where you can indeed feel free: free even to jump untethered from the highest bridge in the city if that is your intention.

131

Notorious is the only word to describe the bridge that we passed under many times as we cruised the lake. The actual name of the bridge is the Aurora Street Bridge or the George Washington Memorial Bridge. This bridge is much higher than the Fremont Bridge, high enough to have earned the nickname the suicide bridge.

The half mile, 155 foot-high bridge has been launch pad for thirty-nine people in the past decade. The jumpers regularly sail past the headquarters of Adobe Images, Getty Images, and many of the dot com companies that are located below. Some of these companies have even brought in grief counselors for their employees who have witnessed the jumpers.

According to various accounts, 230 people have jumped since the bridge was built in 1931. What's going on we wondered. Could it be that the predominantly rainy weather in Seattle really can drive a person to the edge and over.

Downstream to the west, a large boat sits wasting away its in the sixth year of a drama that unfolded when the crew pulled in for fuel, filled the tanks, and then pulled dock lines in an attempt to get away without paying. The Coast Guard soon stopped the boat and then found a cargo of marijuana on board. The boat has not moved since. Interesting, to be sure, but nothing could top what I saw on the 22nd of June.

Naked Parade

"Hey you are here for the parade," my friend said. And sure enough, it was my luck to be in

Fremont on June 22 during the summer solstice. This parade is a bizarre rite of Spring called the Annual Fremont Solstice Parade. This event sees a few hundred people bike, rollerblade, skateboard, and walk through the streets of Freemont to celebrate the longest day of the year. What is unique is that they are all naked.

It isn't everyday that you see about 700 people in the nude with body paint daubed on in strategic places marching in the streets. Some wore costumes, others rode in bizarrely decorated automobiles, most were naked. I loved every minute of it.

And I loved Seattle but after three weeks something was itching my feet and those feet seemed to be pointing north. During my stay in Seattle I had been trying to contact a guy I know who works at Wreck Beach in Vancouver. I thought that since I was close I would go up and visit him.

With some web searching I learned that a ferry leaves Bellingham bound for Skagway every Friday and this got me thinking about a longer trip. That feeling to move was on me again but I did not take the ferry, I caught instead an Amtrak train headed north for Vancouver. Little did I know, as the train sped north beside dramatic mountains and crashing Pacific waves, just how far north I would go.

Vancouver

The train out of Seattle, north along the coast, offered great views of Bald Eagles feeding along the shore, towering mountains, and spruce covered hills. We reached Vancouver and were stalled for two hours on arrival but finally we left the train and went through customs. Two Canadian Customs officials took an unusual interest in me and conducted a thorough inspection of my luggage. The grim-faced man and woman seemed determined to find something as they conducted an inspection of every detail of my luggage. After nearly an hour their grimaces turned to smiles, they apologized for the delay, and they welcomed me to Canada.

I headed towards Chinatown and a hostel I had found there a few years ago through the Lonely Planet guidebook; I had stayed there on a previous trip. Once settled, I left the hostel and headed towards Starbucks for a cup of coffee. On the way I passed a coffee shop and recognized the owner who was standing in the doorway. He was a South African man that I once met on a trip.

"Best coffee in Vancouver," he assured me so I went in and had coffee with him while we chatted. He mentioned Kenny's Kitchen in Chinatown for the best lunch menu in the area. They cater to the local Chinese population and dish out a sumptuous feast spread out on a long, hot-tray table. I headed there next and found that they served every authentic Chinese dish imaginable. The food was good and inexpensive.

In the afternoon I toured the old, three and four story warehouse district, now converted to commercial space and housing along the waterfront.

In the late afternoon I went into an ice cream stand and while I had a dish of homemade vanilla I chatted with the owner. He told me that he used vanilla extract from Mexico to make his vanilla ice cream. When I told him that I spend part of my winters in Mexico he brought out a bottle of Mexican vanilla extract to show me. We chatted about vanilla and some of the extracts made from the Tonka bean, not true vanilla.

True vanilla extract comes from the bean of an orchid that was first found growing on the east facing slopes of the mountains in the town of Papantla, in what is now Veracruz State, along the Gulf of Mexico. I visited there in the past and was reminded of the smell of vanilla in the air in the main plaza of Papantla.

The Orchid is fertilized by a particular insect that lives only in the Papantla area. It took years for the growers to learn the trick of artificially fertilizing the flowers so that vanilla could be grown in other countries. Still the process of propagating the plant and then extracting the vanilla is tedious and labor intensive.

With my memories of Papantla and the scent of vanilla in the air I doubly enjoyed that vanilla ice cream cone that afternoon.

Wreck Beach

The next day I caught the UBC bus which goes to the University of British Colombia. The Wreck Beach is located below the cliffs behind the university's Museum of Anthropology. The bus dropped me near the rose garden which is across from the museum and I spent some time admiring the roses in full bloom. I then walked across the street to the museum to look at the collection of totem poles. From there I walked to the stairs and pathway leading to Wreck Beach.

The climb down the steep cliff among the huge evergreens was strenuous such that I didn't know if I would make it back up. Signs along the way announced Wreck Beach as nude optional. I finally reached the beach where logs had been washed ashore from the river logging operations. These logs made handy seats and shelters for the visitors.

I inquired at the vendor stands about my friend and I found him at the south end of the beach hanging with a group of artists and retirees. After some small talk about mutual acquaintances and their travels, he told me about his latest project. He was building a raft from salvaged beach logs and atop the raft, which was now in a cove secured to shore, he was building a house. If anyone could pull that off I know it would be him; he is a talented carpenter and I have seen projects that he worked on when he winters at Zipolite Beach in Oaxaca Mexico. He is also an accomplished harmonica player who entertains the patrons at the Zipolite watering holes.

Camping Wreck Beach

Later my friend showed me a place along the shore where I could pitch a tent. It was wild camping and not strictly legal but the next day I moved from the hostel to camp in the woods above the beach for a few days.

From the cliffs we could see endless rafts of logs that were being towed along the Fraser River to the wood mills where they would be cut into construction lumber.

The wildness of this land appealed to me and I wanted more. I knew by now that I was headed north but I could never have guessed just how far north I would go.

Vancouver Island

I left Vancouver by BC Ferry and visited Vancouver Island. I spent a day and night in the park and visited the museum to see more totem poles. From there I visited the Hotel Victoria for coffee and to look at the antique furniture. I collect Persian carpets and this elegant old hotel had a great collection.

While I was waiting in Victoria for the one-car train to Courtenay a Japanese guy with a tour group insisted on cutting in line. The conductor stopped him and they nearly came to blows. I had bought coffee and pastry and just stood sipping coffee while I watched the pushing and arguing. Finally the Japanese guy took his place at the back of the line.

I was glad it ended peacefully; no way did I want to witness a murder or to see mounties lug the Japanese guy off to jail. I would deal with my own line jumper later.

In Courtenay I toured around and read about an interesting electrical device submerged in the river that keeps the seals from going upstream to eat the salmon. As wild as the place seemed, they still managed to protect certain animals and birds.

Port Hardy

Later I went to the hotel where I met an English woman who gave me a ride to the bus station for Port Hardy, a fishing village and Coast Guard port with a large harbor full of recreational boats further north on Victoria Island. After a long bus ride through forested country I arrived in Port Hardy. In the early afternoon I walked the beach looking at dozens of bald eagles as I poked around the tide pools. The place was so serene and full of raw nature that I spent the afternoon in the midst of bald eagles as I hunted the pools for starfish and crabs.

I then went to the commercial dock to watch the fishing fleet unload their catch. While indigenous labor worked the docks, a government inspector recorded the catch which consisted mostly of cod. While I was there a guy offered me a whole salmon, free, but I declined and thanked him. Huge, black ravens swarmed about and darted in for any scrap. I got a good look at their beaks and realized that a bite from them would put a hole in you.

At this point with eagles and salmon, ravens and snow-capped peaks all around me I was overwhelmed by excitement at the sight of raw nature and I wanted more. It was an itch deep in my brain to see more of the north. How far north I didn't know, but north.

At Port Hardy I booked the BC Ferry that heads to Prince Rupert on the inland waterway that runs up the coast all the way to Skagway. Once on the ferry and underway, we cruised north on Queen

Charlotte Sound and into the middle of stunning raw nature. Seals and whales, orcas, and water birds were all around us as we cruised for 500 miles beneath the shadow of towering mountains and glaciers. Not a city in sight, just soaring mountains with snow capped peaks, cascades of water flowing down through the lush green forest of Sitka Spruce, and bald eagles feeding along the shore. This was what I wanted; this was what I needed, a couple of days in raw nature, a natural paradise. It was then that I decided to continue north.

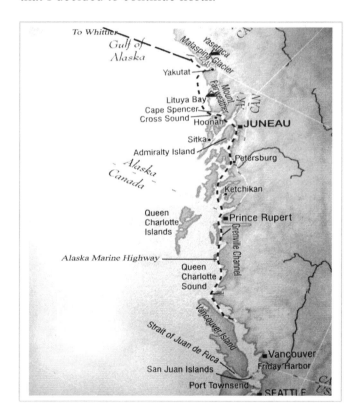

"No eternal reward will forgive us now for wasting the dawn."
— Jim Morrison

"Two roads diverged in a wood and I took the one less traveled by." **Robert Frost**

14. Prince Rupert

My interlude with pristine nature ended with a jolt of reality when we entered Prince Rupert and cruised past the Ridley Coal Terminal.

I imagined the legs of a giant water spider but it wasn't one of natures creatures that greeted me. I was looking at the steel conveyor booms of the coal terminal that juts into the bay to ship over 8 million metric tons of coal annually to China.

Canada built this ice-free, deep-water harbor as the closest port in North America to Asia. Coal comes to Prince Rupert via Canadian Nation Railway, originally from the Quintette and Bullmoose mines, located at Tumblar Ridge in Northeast British Colombia, and then from other mines in BC and Alberta when the first mines shut down.

Prince Rupert also handles container cargo and the harbor terminal exports grain and lumber.

I left the boat and went along the river to find the hostel where I had a reservation. Once settled in, I noticed that the hostel's gas fired kitchen stove needed a good cleaning so I bought some supplies and went to work. When the owner returned and saw what I had done she was so appreciative that she wanted to feed me at no cost for the duration of my stay.

The visitors, most under 30, were an international collection that included Brits, Dutch, French, and Australians. I hooked up with a few of them and we made the best we could of Prince Rupert but most visitors were in transit and there was not much to do there except gambling and beach combing.

Several ferries serve Prince Rupert, including a once a month ferry that goes north up channel to Ketchikan, Petersburg, Kake, and then across the open ocean to Whittier. I knew now that my hikers needed to crunch the ice and snow as they had done in Antarctica; I booked passage to Whittier Alaska.

Alaska Marine Highway

I read about the Alaska Marine Highway system during my stay in Seattle. When I reached Prince Rupert and realized that there was three months of summer left, I had to book a cruise to Alaska.

Departure day came and I shared a taxi to the ferry terminal with another traveler heading north. When we arrived as, "walk-ons," they seemed delighted to see us. We never did find out why walk-ons were so welcome as we headed through US Customs where they checked for fruit. I had some food with me for the three-day trip but they had no problem with apples and nuts, oatmeal, raisins, and sandwiches. We headed for the top deck at the back of the ship where there was a heated sitting room.

Many people pitch a tent on deck and secure it with duck tape against the wind but it must be placed outside, not under the roofed portions of the ship. I didn't want to deal with pitching a tent in the winds on an open deck so I planned to sleep on a bench on top of my mat in my sleeping bag under the cover of the roofed deck. There was just one other traveler there, a writer from the US who was working on a story about Alaska.

Ships

The ships carry automobiles, campers, and trucks in a lower vehicle deck. Passengers have a choice of staterooms or deck space to pitch a tent. At night the ship showed movies and during the day a ranger lectured about the whales and seals that we saw and about the animals and birds we might encounter in Alaska.

These ships cruise along the coast and visit the small villages as part of the Alaska Marine Highway. They supply villages like Ketchikan, Petersburg, Kake, and Juneau where no roads lead out from the coast to connect to highways and the larger cities; everything comes in by ship or air.

Juneau
We docked at Juneau which is the capital of the State of Alaska although the city has no road out beyond the coastal mountains to connect with the State of Alaska's road and highway system. Our landfall was 25 miles outside of the village center so I hitched in to find a store; I needed a few items including a corkscrew.

I arrived in Juneau and was astounded to see that the town clung to a tiny shelf of land beneath towering mountains. I found my corkscrew and hitched back to the boat. Hitchhiking is easy in Alaska - usually.

We then headed for Whittier by way of stops at Pelican and Yakutat. The boat cruised through narrow channels rimmed by snow-capped mountains with streams of melt water cascading down into the lush green bases of the mountains and into the ocean channel. The 20 hours of daylight resulted in warm temperatures during the day and mild nights. The further north we went the longer the hours of daylight became. After Yakutat we entered the open ocean and cruised all day and night on smooth seas across the Gulf of Alaska to Whittier.

We entered Whittier in the rain. Once the ship docked we took the stairs down to the vehicle deck to exit by the ramp. As I left the ship I noticed a five seated bicycle, something I had never seen before. During my walk to the port office to arrange transportation to Homer, the five seated bicycle passed me with the father in the front seat, the mother in the back seat, and three small children peddling away in the middle.

A five-seated bicycle with mother in the back, father in the front, and three children in the middle prepares to leave Whittier.

"Reality leaves a lot to the imagination."
— John Lennon

"As soon as you trust yourself, you will know how to live."
Johann Wolfgang von Goethe

15. Whittier

It is about 130 miles from Whittier to Homer so I inquired about a van that makes a regular run. I was told that the van would pick me up on the other side of the tunnel where a group of buildings stands near the highway. The tunnel is a five-mile cut through a mountain that the US Army built during World War II for freight trains when Whittier was a submarine base.

The tunnel has one way traffic with a light system so I walked to the entrance and then went down the line of cars asking for a lift. The first vehicle was a pickup and the guy gave me a flat no. Ditto the rest of the cars. I went back to the pickup and walked the line again as more cars arrived and still I got a no.

On my third attempt, the pickup driver rolled down his window and hollered, "Get in," as he motioned towards the back bed of the pickup. I jumped in just as the light changed and soon we were through the tunnel. He took me the length of Portage Glacier Road to Route One, the road to Homer. I jumped out and headed for the group of buildings near the road but saw that there were two groups of buildings near two different roads. I chose the wrong highway I realized when I caught sight of the van on the other road as it quickly disappeared in the direction of Homer. I waved and hollered but it was futile as the taillights faded from view on Route 1 towards Homer. I started to walk.

Hitchhiking to Homer
Having missed the van I had two choices, go back to Whittier or make this an adventure and walk to Homer. I had no intention of walking all the way when I started out in the direction of Homer; hitchhiking is easy in Alaska I assured myself.

For miles and miles cars passed me but none offered a lift. I continued walking while still telling myself that hitchhiking in Alaska is easy and that soon someone would stop. After about 10 miles of walking, however, my legs told me that it was time for a rest and I realized that I was stranded.

This was indeed going to be an adventure as I started looking for a place to pitch a tent.

The sides of the roads looked inviting enough but upon walking into the woods I found soft and mushy tundra that would not be suitable for the pitching of a tent. I continued walking and eventually came to a small waterfall and a stream that ran under the road. I found a flat dry spot near the pool below the falls and set up my tent.

Before long an Indian man and his wife stopped at the pool to clean some salmon they had caught. I said hello and then watched as the man carefully cleaned the fish and bagged up the entrails. Unusual for a fisherman to be so fastidious with the fish guts I thought so I asked him why he didn't just dump the viscera in the stream like most fishermen do.

"Bears," he said, "I don't want them coming around your tent and neither do you."

I was struck by that thoughtfulness and then I started to think about bears.

"Do I need to worry about bears," I asked.

"Yes," he said, "and I don't like to see you alone in the woods. I would offer a ride but I don't have enough gas to make Homer."

They insisted on taking me to Homer if I helped with the gas but I thanked them and declined the offer, though kind it was; I didn't want them to go so far out of their way. Meanwhile the man's wife handed me two bottles of water and a package of cupcakes. "Take the water," she said, "we are going home and we don't need it." I had asked them earlier about drinking the stream water but I knew it was not a good practice in the wild because Giardia can be a problem even in pristine streams of Alaska where many animals feed.

I tied my food high in a tree a good distance from my tent and I had no trouble with bears that night. I would have my run in with a bear much later.

The next morning I woke to the sound of people near the falls. I was soon up and walking the road and within minutes, a pickup screamed to a stop and backed up to offer a lift. He was on his way to Seward, the town named after the man who bought Alaska from the Russians. As he drove we chatted about Alaskan history.

Sewards Ice Box

William H. Seward was Secretary of State under Abraham Lincoln and later President Andrew Johnson. He served first as Governor of New York, the man told me, and then Secretary of State in the Lincoln cabinet. He was an ardent anti-slavery advocate and was the victim of an assassination attempt by one of John Wilkes

150

Booth's accomplices. He survived several knife wounds and continued his duties in the cabinet under Andrew Johnson.

Seward advocated the purchase of Alaska from Russia but met derision in the Senate when his plan was labeled, "Sewards Folly," and "Sewards Ice Box."

The Russians owned Alaska and they nearly depleted the territory of the fur-bearing animals, particularly the sea otter. They administered the area loosely while at the same time they feared that their enemy in the Crimean War, Britain, would encroach and edge them out. Rather than give up Alaska to the British and gain nothing, the Russian monarchy offered Alaska to both the US and to Britain in an attempt to drive up the price. While Britain showed no interest, US Secretary of State Seward indulged a worldview that would have the US incorporate all territory in the northern hemisphere including Alaska, British Columbia, Hawaii, Central America, and the Caribbean Islands. Seward finally prevailed and the purchase went through on March 30th of 1867. The 7.2 million that went to the cash-strapped monarchy of Russia looks today, at 2 cents per acre, like a steal.

The road came to a Y and I got out for the road to Homer. I walked for three miles and enjoyed the scenery. In the distance I could see sand cranes and white herons on a lake. When I got closer I stopped on a hill near the lake for a picnic of apples and cheese and I drank the second bottle of gift water while I enjoyed the scene of unspoiled nature before me.

Back on the road, I hooked a ride with a moving van within 30 minutes.

"Was that you pitched by the waterfall," the driver asked, "I passed there last night and saw your tent."

We soon reached Soldotna on the Kenai Peninsula and I was closing in on Homer. I walked to the Kenai River in Soldotna and watched people catching salmon. Later, at the visitors center, I learned that Soldotna holds the record for king Salmon: 97.4 pounds. Nearby the Russian River is famous for Salmon fishing and a well-known gathering place for bears and bald eagles when the salmon are running. I had earlier passed the road to Russian River on the road into Soldotna and was happy that I wasn't walking and camping since every bear in the area had by now converged on the Russian River Salmon run.

Our doubts are traitors and make us lose the good we oft might win by fearing to attempt.
William Shakespeare

16. Homer

I arrived in Homer after a hitch and walked to the $24 USD a night hostel that I found in LP. The manager insisted on several forms of ID but all I had was a passport. He wouldn't budge so I left there and walked to a nearby church where they offered a four-bunk dorm room for $10 a night. The fee included washer dryer, food, and TV sitting room. In return they asked a few chores but did not insist on attendance at religious services. I stayed at the church for a week.

I soon met a fisherman who owned a pickup and we drove out to the Homer Spit each day to fish for salmon. Several nights a week he baked salmon with seasonings for dinner. I don't like salmon, however, so I ate mostly salads or beans and rice.

The church provided donated food for people who came in from the street for dinner. I took to cleaning the kitchen each day as my chore.

During the days that I wasn't fishing I walked the town for recreation and looked at old fishing boats of all description and in all phases of decrepitude. Lupines in the boat yards made colorful contrasts to the weathered wood of derelict boats and rusty fishing gear. Lupines grew in huge swaths everywhere and I often saw moose roaming through fields of lupine at the edge of the woods and on roadsides nearby.

One day I walked the beach and came to a hut made of driftwood. A fire still smoldered in the hearth. I put on some fresh logs and stoked a warming fire and sat for a while to savor some bread from the great bakery in the village and some cheese with a bottle of wine. The hut grew too warm and I went outside and sat for a long while on a log nearby while continuing my picnic lunch. I waited the long afternoon but in vain; the hobbits who lived in the hut never did return.

Van To Seward

A ferry out of Homer used to make stops in Seward but service ended a few years back so I was left with few choices. One option was to book a van for the 150 miles to Seward. Several van lines serve Alaska with 15-passenger vans that haul enclosed trailers behind to carry bikes and backpacks.

I booked a van and within a few hours we reached Seward where fishing and cruise boats crowd into the harbor. The town of 3,000 is remarkable as it hunkers on 14 square miles below towering peaks.

Seward's fishing industry is one of the best in the country in value. Its second successful industry, tourism, is also thriving. Cruise lines dock in Seward and bring tourists who book private rail cars on the Alaska Railroad and travel inland to Denali from the Seward cruise ship dock.

I wanted to visit Seward for a while so I booked a tent site on the beach in town. At the campground I shared my site with a Frenchman who was biking through Alaska. He had flown in with his saddlebags and bought a touring bike for a summer-long trip through the state.

Seward is a bike friendly town and popular stop for bikers in Alaska because of its miles of bike trails. Many European bike riders tour through Seward which does connect to the main highway system of Alaska and allows tourist to visit by train, bus, bike, air, or auto.

Recreational salmon fishing is a popular tourist activity in Seward

"Tourists don't know where they've been, travelers don't know where they're going."   **Paul Theroux**

17. Anchorage

After visiting Seward I took the Alaskan Railway to Anchorage.

The train was a long one with several cars owned by the cruise ship companies, identifiable by their glass dome observation decks. As the rail cars clacked along on the scenic 127-mile trip, I recognized the road on which I walked when I left Whittier. The tracks ran beside Route One, south of Anchorage. The rail line then crossed the Portage Glacier Road where I first started my long walk to Homer.

The train stopped in downtown Anchorage and I began walking to the hostel. After a mile or so I encountered a taxi and I asked the driver if he knew the place.

"Hop in," he said, "I will give you a lift." He was taking a fare to the airport and the kind passenger didn't mind if I tagged along.

After savoring my luck in getting a free cab ride I realized how fleeting fortune can be when the driver dropped me at the hostel and it was full. I was too tired to look further so for $18 a night I pitched a tent on the hostel grounds.

I like the freedom of impromptu travel and don't mind taking my chances with lodging because I know that I will find something, even if it is a rustic tent site.

July was on us at that point and the sun never fully set. It was light for 24 hours. Sleeping was not easy under those conditions and it didn't help that seaplanes were taking off day and night on nearby Lake Hood. I quickly adjusted to the noise, however, and stayed at the hostel for three days.

I took breakfast two of the days in a beautiful old hotel a half mile from the hostel on Lake Hood. There I had a marvelous view of the hundreds of floatplanes that use the lake for an airport while they run fishing and sightseeing trips to the wild lakes of Alaska.

In the evenings I went to the hotel bar to drink and chat with other travelers. From the lounge I sipped gin and tonics and watched the airplanes take off from the lake.

Tidal Bore

The tides in Anchorage are extreme at 35 feet and the local people warn about walking out too far on the flats where a tidal bore that can produce a wave as high as four feet.

I sensed the flavor of this danger one day while walking out on the flats when a kind man operating a container crane near the shore jumped down from his operator's booth and ran towards me shouting and waving his arms to warn me. I learned from him that the water can rush in so fast that anyone too far out on the tidal flats risks drowning. These extreme changes of the tides are due to the town's location deep into the end of the fiord-like Cook Inlet. The fiord ends in a bay called Turnagain Arm, a colorful name that prompted some research.

Local legend tells of the name being applied by William Bligh, the famed Bounty Captain who was on an earlier voyage as Sailing Master for Captain Cook aboard the HMS Resolution. Cook ordered Bligh to search the inlet for a Northwest Passage.

On the first try Bligh found that the arm of water southeast of Anchorage at the end of what is now Cook Inlet came to an abrupt end. Cook wasn't satisfied and ordered a second attempt, thus the name Turnagain Arm.

Perpetual Sunshine

The long days of sunshine in Anchorage cause the flowers to grow huge and brilliant. It was incredible to see dense plantings of nasturtium, begonias showy and lush, outsized zinnias, and huge amaryllis. All of this riotous nature just didn't fit with the concept I had of Alaska, the frozen north.

Lots of fur traders and specialty shops also color the city. These shops will create any article of clothing you want out of beaver, bear, wolf, or moose hide. In Anchorage you can't help but find fur shops and stunning arrays of flowers.

I hiked out along the coast and when I returned I found that the weekend fair had sprung up in the parking lot at the start of the trail. The booths sold food which included caribou hot dogs, huge and delicious. King crab was another specialty. The fair booths also displayed photos of Alaska wildlife for sale by the hundreds; beautiful shots of bears and eagles, moose and musk ox with mountain backgrounds. One photographer's specialty was photos of the northern lights and he had some stunning shots including one that won a magazine contest. He took the photo in April with a camera of his own design.

Inuit Skinning Knife

Two articles that you might not find anywhere else in the world interested me. One was a knife of a special design that the Eskimos have used since 2500 BC. The knife shape has changed little since prehistoric times and now has become a collectors item for tourists. The Inuit skinning knife has a curved blade and a handle that runs between the two ends of the blade.

The original knife was called an Ulu. It is still used by the Inuit women for the skinning of seals and fur bearing animals. The Inuit use Ulus of various sizes for all sorts of chores including food preparation and even sewing. Now the knife in many iterations is collected by visitors to Alaska.

Qiviut

The second item of interest to me was the many winter-ready articles of clothing made by the Inuit women from the fur of the musk ox.

The musk ox appears to be a bison-like animal about the size of a Shetland pony but is actually more closely related to sheep. The animal migrated to Alaska from Siberia 90,000 years ago but was hunted to extinction in Alaska during the 1850s gold rush. Musk ox was reintroduced into Alaska in the 1950s from wild Canadian stock. I saw several herds on Alaskan farms in my travels.

The Inuit adopted the production of clothing articles from the musk ox fur as a cottage industry. They learned their knitting skills from missionaries. The Inuit now make the warm clothing by combing the under fur of the musk ox and harvesting fibers that they call qiviut. The qiviut is reputed to be finer than cashmere, yet stronger and eight times warmer than the wool of sheep even when wet. The fibers cause no allergic reactions and can be washed with no shrinkage. The Inuit women spin the fibers and make yarn from the fir with which they knit shawls, scarves, hats, and mittens. They do not use looms but use needlework to make these warm articles of clothing now prized as, "The Cashmere of the North."

This much sought-after knitted clothing from the musk ox tempted me; I wanted an Inuit pullover hat but reality struck; I am always leaving things behind in my travels and these unique wool items were pricey; I had to pass.

I continued my tour of Anchorage and marveled at the brilliant begonias, nasturtiums, zinnias, and amaryllis outside the Visitors Center. The museum-like building was full of Indian lore, stuffed animals, wildlife photos, and Native American artifacts.

Fairbanks

After a few days of touring Anchorage, I booked a ticket on the Alaska Railway for a train that left Anchorage and headed towards Fairbanks. I checked out of the hostel and took a campsite near the train station to be ready for the morning departure. Next day I boarded the train and settled in for a scenic trip.

In one of the cars, a naturalist described the scenery and pointed out the wildlife that we encountered which included three black bear, several moose with young, a male moose with a rack, and many migratory birds. We passed through Wassila and then stopped at Talkeetna where I left the train. I walked to the Susitna River and sat for a long while by the shore where I had a view of Mount McKinley to the north. Denali was my next stop.

"Every wall is a door." Ralph Waldo Emerson

18. He Died With His Boots On

Talkeetna is a staging area for climbers of Mount McKinley. I booked into the hostel where many climbers waited their turn on the mountain. Most of them were forced to acclimate for two or three weeks before their ascent. Once their turn came they would shuttle to the airport for a flight to the McKinley base camp.

Mount McKinley

Mount McKinley at 20,320 feet (6194m) presents challenges to the climber, especially since it is located in the coldest part of the northern hemisphere and has seen winter temperatures as low as −75 degrees Fahrenheit. (-59.44 C)

While I was in Talkeetna, I was reminded of the danger when two Japanese climbers died on the mountain. And in fact over one hundred climbers have died since the first ascent in 1913. On entering the graveyard in Talkeetna I saw a plaque that list the names of those that have perished while climbing McKinley. One marker displayed a pair of sculpted stone hiking boots above the epitaph, "He Died With His Boots On."

Talkeetna is a picturesque town where you find good views of Mount McKinley. Many cruise ship passengers arrive at the train station in Talkeetna on their way to Denali National Park.

Denali National Park

After my stay at Talkeetna I booked a seat on a train to Denali. The train's destination was Fairbanks but there are several stops along the way including the Denali station where I found hotels and campgrounds and the bus service into the park.

Cruise passengers come up from Seward and Whittier by train and continue into the park by bus. No cars can enter Denali NP and in summer the park can fill. At times the number of people allowed to enter by bus is limited.

I went into the visitors center to book a bus trip and enjoyed the great views out over a canyon that had been carved by a glacier. The visitors center offers all sorts of activities including hiking, animal lore, animal awareness information, bus trips, dogsled rides, and gold panning. The treat for bus passenger is to see the big four of Denali wildlife: wolf, caribou, bear, and moose. On the bus ride I saw all four.

After my bus trip I camped for two nights in a treed campsite with nearby bathroom, shower, and site fireplace. From Denali I caught a train to Fairbanks.

While waiting in the ticket line to purchase train passage to Fairbanks a rude tourist tried to cut in line ahead of me.

"Hey, I was here before you," I hollered, "There is a line here and it starts back there,"

Fresh on my mind was the day I was patient with line cutters only to reach the ticket window and find the trains sold out. It cost me another night in a hotel and a wasted day so I was not going to put up with people cutting in line. I have gotten used to rude people cutting in line on many trips in Mexico and India where they just don't pay attention to lines. The big boned ladies and the young men in Mexico will try to cut the line whenever they think they can get away with it. When you call them on it they just apologize as if it was a mistake. From that day that I missed my train connection because of a line jumper, I have had no tolerance for people who do it. The guy backed off and soon I reached the ticket window.

With a ticket for Fairbanks I was aboard the train comfortably watching the incredible Alaska scenery through my picture window. We stopped at one place so passengers could photograph a huge glacier.

Fairbanks

We reached Fairbanks in the rain and I took a cab to a hostel that I had found in LP. The hostel was full so I moved on and found Billie's Backpacker Hostel, a white building with red trim that offered plenty of space and included a teepee for rent outside. I chose the teepee and shared it with a German guy who was biking through Alaska.

I stayed at Billie's Hostel for a week. I found it a great place that offered all I needed: free WiFi, free storage, coin-op laundry, books, maps, and a friendly owner who even offered free bikes for the use of her guests.

To keep busy during the morning I cleaned up around the place and I chatted occasionally with Billie. She suggested a van service that ran trips to the North Slope and I was sorely tempted. I had not planned to go to Prudhoe Bay but the lure of wading in the Arctic Ocean became irresistible.

I had already followed Route 190, the Pan American Highway, all the way south and beyond to take a swim in an Antarctic volcanic lagoon, why not complete the trip and follow 190 all the way north. Why not dunk in the ocean as far north as I could go.

Prudhoe Bay via the Dalton Highway or "Haul Road" as they called it looked like a must do but the trip was pricey at 700 USD. I needed to give it some thought.

Diversion came my way at Billie's. One day a guest returned from a blueberry picking morning with two gallons of berries. He baked up a cobbler, a pie, and some muffins for all to share and we gorged on blueberry pastries. Later that day we walked to the river to watch the Rubber Ducky Contest, a quirky event that included the dumping of hundreds of rubber ducks into the Salena River. The first duck to reach the finish line down river won the grand prize. The person who purchased that ticket and had their number affixed to that duck won some cash. The proceeds went to a charitable cause and everyone had fun.

I got involved in another odd-ball event when I helped a French couple build a raft that they used to float down the river in a contest to see who could make the most unusual raft. Theirs was a unique raft indeed when they mounted their bikes atop the raft and launched into the river astride their bikes. They pedaled as if they were providing locomotion but the river provided the motive force while my friends and a fleet of quirky rafts passed the judging stands. My friends didn't win the raft contest but we all had some laughs putting the raft together.

The event ended in a park where the contestants were served breakfast We all took in a gold panning exhibition and handled huge nuggets of gold that came out of the mountains.

A highlight for me each day was to ride my bike, courtesy of Billie's, to a great breakfast shack a mile from the hostel where I could gorge on sourdough pancakes. Another good trip was a ride to the University of Alaska campus for a tour of the museum, a hike in the large park with a view of McKinley, and a look at a captive herd of musk ox, animals that were descendants of the reintroduction herd from Canada.

As I rode the bike all over Fairbanks, I couldn't help but think about my year of travel. Last year I was at the bottom of the earth and this year I was at the top, why not go as far north as I can, why not go to Prudhoe Bay and dip my toes in the Beaufort Sea.

I called the van service that Billie recommended and booked a ticket to Prudhoe Bay and the Arctic Ocean. The van pulled up at six in the morning a few days later and off we went to run to the northern end of Route 190 on the Dalton Highway.

"All that is gold does not glitter, not all those who wander are lost."
J. R. R. Tolkien

19. The Haul Road

Three of us rode in the van, four counting the driver. That made the minimum number of passengers with which the van will make the two-day trip.

We first stopped at a sign outside of town for photos and orientation. The big green James W Dalton Highway sign where we posed for photos was festooned with mementos and flag decals left by national and international visitors. It seems that the Haul Road has become a 500-mile right of passage for world travelers.

Dalton Highway

An advisory instructed us to carry two spare tires and to expect that our windshield would take a rock thrown up by truck tires. We looked at the oil pipeline and at the "Pig" that is sent through the pipe periodically to clean wax from the inside wall of the pipe.

We headed out on the 500-mile gravel highway after reading instructions that we should pull over for oil company equipment. We did encounter some strange looking rigs headed towards Prudhoe and returning. Our driver became our guide and he explained much about the pipeline.

One of the few road signs we saw, about 80 miles out, told the story: Yukon River 56, Cold Foot 175, Dead Horse 414.

We crossed the Arctic Circle. At that point and beyond to the north, on the June solstice, the sun would remain above the horizon for twenty-four hours. Conversely, on December 22, it would not rise at all.

We stopped at Cold Foot to gas up. A smorgasbord restaurant at the stop offered food but the other passengers, a couple from the US, and I, knew ahead of the trip that it was expensive so we had brought our own food.

Pipeline

Our driver explained that the oil company owns the road and that they built it in record time between 1974 and 1977 to service the 48 inch pipeline that runs 800 miles from the North

170

Slope at Prudhoe Bay to the oil terminal at Valdez. The Trans-Alaska Pipeline System, dubbed TAPS, is an engineering marvel with 11 pumping stations placed at 75 mile intervals along the main pipeline route and hundreds of miles of pipelines in the North Slope oil fields that feed into the main line. The cost of construction including the Valdez Ship Terminal was eight billion dollars.

The pipeline has leaked on occasion and our driver recounted a story with an amusing twist. It seems that a drunken man once shot a hole in the pipeline. His vandalism caused a six thousand-barrel oil spill and he was arrested and sentenced to jail for 16 years. This unfortunate man from Livengood Alaska was also ordered to pay for the cleanup: 17 million dollars.

We saw few signs on the road. As we went deeper, the landscape turned to nearly treeless tundra broken only by the pipeline and an occasional pumping station.

The pipeline is elevated above ground for the most part because the heat of the oil within the pipe would melt the permafrost if the pipes were buried. At places we saw where the pipes went below ground and there we saw heat-dissipating fins rising from the earth. Their purpose was to conduct the heat from the metal pipe away from the earth and prevent the melting of the permafrost.

Beaufort Sea

After a full day of driving we reached Deadhorse and Prudhoe Bay. We checked in for a tour.

Security is tight at the entrance where we showed ID and paid thirty dollars to enter.

We learned that more than five oil fields send oil to the pipeline through feeder pipes. Natural geologic pressures push the oil up from the wells 10,000 feet below the surface at 120 degrees Fahrenheit and it begins to cool as it passes through various processes to separate water, natural gas, and other elements. It then feeds into the 48-inch pipeline where it enters at 110 degrees. Almost one million barrels a day, equaling 42 million gallons of oil, flow through the pipeline. This, however, is well below its two million- barrel capacity. The oil is then sent on its way south and takes nearly 12 days to reach Valdez.

Purdhoe Bay

Three thousand workers run the Prudhoe Bay oil fields in rotating shifts of two weeks, seven days a week, 12 hours a day on duty. They then get two weeks off. The workers ship back to Fairbanks on a pair of oil company Boing 737s that make 5 trips a day. The airliners have flight attendants on board who serve meals and drinks but alcohol is served only on the way to Fairbanks, not on the return to Prudhoe.

We saw specialized equipment on the site, trucks with huge tires that can roll over the tundra without damaging it. Legend has it that a man was run over by one of these vehicles and it caused no injury.

Part of the tour was a trip to the edge of the Beaufort Sea where tourists often wade into the water and even swim. In the distance we could see the arctic ice sheet.

I don't like the cold all that much but I couldn't help myself; I had to wade in. The cold water brought back memories of my Antarctic swim. Now I had dunked in both the Arctic and the Antarctic oceans.

After the tour and swim we left Prudhoe Bay and cruised through the town of Deadhorse where we saw a wild herd of musk ox and a caribou herd. We were headed south now towards the town of Wiseman, still north of the Arctic Circle, where we would put into a hotel for the night. After a couple hours drive we crossed the great divide and reached Wiseman, a quaint village off the Dalton Highway. We passed into the town through the arched gateway formed of moose and caribou horn. After settling into the hotel we looked over the many artifacts in the general store.

Along the same stretch of road we earlier met Pierre, a French Canadian man who was an ardent walker. Early in the year he set out to walk to Prudhoe Bay from Vancouver while tenting along the way. He loaded his gear onto a three-wheeled cart and when we met him he was nearly at the North Slope. I ran into him again in Fairbanks.

We completed the southbound trip on the haul road and returned to Fairbanks. In Fairbanks I booked a seat on a van that was headed towards Whitehorse. I planned to leave the van at the road through Eagle and from there reach Dawson City.

While I was waiting for the van I met Pierre again, pushing his three-wheeled cart. He had reached Prudhoe and then caught a van back from the North Slope.

We piled in the van and off towards Whitehorse we went, Pierre on his way to Whitehorse and me bound for an intersection just beyond the village of Tok. At that intersection I planned to leave the van and take the road to Eagle and then take a riverboat to Dawson City.

All was going so well I could never have imagined that before long I would find myself stranded in a three-store, gold panning town called Chicken.

"O public road, I say back, I am not afraid to leave you, yet I love you, you express me better than I can express myself."
Walt Whitman

20. Stranded In Chicken

The shortest way to Dawson City from Tok was through the small, former gold-mining village of Chicken. This seasonal road was via Route 5, a gravel road. The route would then be towards Eagle on the Yukon River or on Route 9 which splits off before Eagle and goes into Canada to Dawson City.

The reasoning for my trip to Eagle was to catch a boat on the Yukon River to Dawson City rather than go by road. I wanted to see the Gold Rush memorabilia and to experience a Yukon River ferry trip. I never could have imagined what a washed out road would do to my plans. Rather than enjoying a few days in Eagle and a trip up the Yukon River, I would find myself hopelessly stranded in that tiny, gold-panning village called Chicken.

This plan of mine had its start at Billie's Hostel in Fairbanks when I met a man who traveled with a small poodle dog while he did some prospecting and panning for gold in Eagle. The man told me about the boat out of Eagle that took tourist up river to Dawson City. That sounded like a great trip and it started me on the road for Eagle.

The plan was to reach Tok and then find another van that ran the road through the village of Chicken and on to the town of Eagle.

I started off and when I reached Tok I met a van driver that I had met earlier. He was on his way to Whitehorse and he offered to drop me at the intersection for the road to Eagle. I left his van near the intersection of Route 2 and Route 5 and walked in the rain to the start of Route 5 towards Chicken and Eagle. On the walk I noticed no traffic in either direction on the road to Chicken and Eagle. I decided that my only option at that point was to hunker down and wait for the van that ran to Eagle.

Within ten minutes, however, a pickup truck hauling a fifth-wheel camping trailer stopped to pick me up. The driver was an engineer from Fairbanks who was heading for the village of Chicken where he was testing water for the State.

After 60 miles the man dropped me at the crossroads to his campground, about a mile outside of the village center. I started walking down a long gentle slope and into a valley where I found the Village of Chicken.

Chicken

They call it a village but really we are talking three stores, a restaurant, curio shop, gas station, and liquor store. A few scattered houses and a campgrounds and that is it.

I went into the restaurant and ordered coffee. I took the coffee out on the porch and talked to a few local people. They told me that the road to Eagle was washed out. Sure enough I saw a barricade in the distance with a road closed sign. Now I knew why there had been so little traffic on the road to Eagle.

After a few inquiries I found that various people had various opinions on how long the road would be closed. Those opinions ranged from a few days to a month. I inquired about a campsite.

The man who I had met in Fairbanks with the poodle pulled in. He was on his way to eagle. I thought I was in luck but he had his truck full to the brim with mining supplies and provisions so he could not take me. He planned to skirt the barricade and try to make it to Eagle regardless of the road closed sign.

I visited the campgrounds and found a collection of summer prospectors who came to Chicken to pan for gold in Chicken Creek. I walked the creek for a mile and found a good flat place for a tent. There was only one option left to me, to set up my tent and settle in for the night.

The rains came harder during the night and I worried that the creek might rise and flood me out. In the morning I found that indeed the creek was running full but I still had plenty of campsite left. I sat outside my tent enjoying the scenery regardless of a light drizzle and was astonished to see a bull moose with a huge rack emerge from the brush and come to the waters edge opposite me for a drink. He didn't see me or he just didn't care, I don't know but he stood for a long while not fifty feet from me. He turned and went back into the brush and I could hear him tearing up the shrubbery for his morning meal.

When I went into the restaurant for breakfast I learned that the road had been further damaged during the rainy night and would be closed for at least a week. It hit me then that I was indeed stranded in Chicken.

That turn of events prompted me to do some research.

Chicken: settled 1850, population 17, density, one person per square mile, distance to the next town 100 miles, principle form of entertainment, panning for gold.

Panning For Gold

When in Chicken do as the Chickenites do. I walked Chicken Creek and panned for nuggets. I sat on the porch of the restaurant with an old prospector and watched nothing happen. I walked to the old Pedro Dredge and looked it over. I sat on the porch some more with the old prospector and talked about nothing. I walked to the campgrounds and watched the campers pan for gold. I talked again to the old prospector.

When I talked about gold he talked about the weather. When I asked about the sluice box that he had back in the woods, he talked about the drizzle. I knew that he must have been finding some gold but we talked best when we talked about nothing. A few more questions from me and he went silent. I had no choice then but to watch for a bus that I knew would never come.

The roads were washed out and the usual tourist buses would not be coming to Chicken nor would they travel the hundred miles to the north to the town of Eagle. The buses and vans out of Anchorage would be going to Dawson by first going to Whitehorse in Canada and then going back north to Dawson, a detour of about eight hundred miles. I was stuck in Chicken.

Grizzly

Late in the afternoon I headed for my tent and put in a good nights sleep. Some time in the morning before sunrise a noise outside my tent startled me. I sat up and I heard a slap on the side of my tent.

"Hey, who is it," I hollered but there was no answer. I opened the tent front and stepped out into semidarkness and drizzle. I didn't see anyone.

As I stood up, I looked behind me on the other side of the tent and there stood a huge

179

grizzly bear. The sight shocked me and I froze. He rose up on his hind legs as he turned towards me and he looked at me with tiny brown eyes.

It came back to me in a flash what to do. I remembered what all the posters and advisories had said. I stood still. I then stood as tall as I could and slowly raised my arms over my head.

"Hey bear," I said in a low voice, "Hey bear, take it easy bear."

He just stood and looked at me. I continued talking to him and I couldn't help but remember what an old Indian man once said to me.

"If you are camping out in Alaska you will meet a bear, you had better be careful with your food. These bears will eat you."

"Hey bear," I continued, "Take it easy bear." He just stood looking at me. We looked eye to eye for the longest time and then he calmly dropped to all fours. I thought it was all over for me then but the bear turned and in seconds he disappeared into the brush.

After a few minutes I looked at the lower front fly of my tent and found four new holes, perfect bear claw-sized holes.

I went up to the restaurant for breakfast and told the owner about my encounter. She in a matter of fact voice told me that they see bear all the time around the store. She then offered me a wood-floor tent behind the store if I was willing to clean it up. I could stay there for free if I cleaned it. Within minutes I was in the cabin and sprucing up the place. I moved in that afternoon.

New Home

The tent had a fireplace so I started a fire and hung my tent to dry. Before long the cabin was toasty warm and too warm for me after sleeping outside for three days. The fire died down eventually and I slept well.

The following day I visited the restaurant for breakfast and took my coffee out to the porch where I met the old prospector again.

I mentioned again that I would like to see his sluice operation but he was having none of that. He steered the conversation to his favorite subject and we again talked about nothing.

With nothing to do I walked again to the derelict Pedro gold dredge. It was usually open for tours but since the road was closed there were no tourists and no tours.

I walked the creek again. Panning gold occupied some afternoon time but it proved futile. I walked to the store again and I sat on the porch. The old prospector saw me coming and he skulked off into the woods. I sat down and again I looked for a bus that I knew would never arrive.

"Even people whose lives have been made various by learning sometimes find it hard to keep a fast hold on their habitual views of life, on their faith in the Invisible - nay, on the sense that their past joys and sorrows are a real experience, when they are suddenly transported to a new land, where the beings around them know nothing of their history, and share none of their ideas - where their mother earth shows another lap, and human life has other forms than those on which their souls have been nourished.

Minds that have been unhinged from their old faith and love have perhaps sought this Lethean influence of exile in which the past becomes dreamy because its symbols have all vanished, and the present too is dreamy because it is linked with no memories."

George Eliot, Silas Marner

"Though we travel the world over to find the beautiful, we must carry it with us or we find it not." Ralph Waldo Emerson

21. Escaping Chicken

Early the next morning the restaurant owner knocked on my door and said that a guy in the restaurant was looking for a driver to help him reach Dawson City. Was I interested? Sounded to me as if a miraculous escape from Chicken was in the offing so I was up and dressed in minutes.

The guy was in the restaurant having breakfast so I joined him. He was transporting mining equipment and had planned to reach Dawson in the Yukon Territory of Canada through the town of Chicken, usually a six hour trip. The road washout, however, had stopped him in Chicken. He planned to drive 64 miles back out to the main highway and take a 380 mile detour, south to Whitehorse and then back north 330 miles to Dawson. Would I help with the driving? Even though it was an 800 mile trip, I jumped at the chance. I would have done anything to escape from Chicken.

We were soon on the road out of Chicken with me driving and the guy sound asleep in the front seat of the diesel pickup hauling a fifth-wheel trailer full of mining equipment.

I was just getting my driving chops in order when a caribou bolted from the bushes and stood in the middle of the road in front of me. He just stood there looking at the chrome bumper of a dual-wheel diesel headed his way. I hit the brakes softly, as the man had instructed me before he fell asleep, fully prepared to also hit the caribou rather than splay mining equipment all over the Taylor Highway to Chicken. Luckily the caribou leaped into the woods just before I would have nailed his furry behind. The guy mumbled something and then went back to sleep and I continued on over the seasonal road toward Tetlin Junction with a little less pressure on the gas peddle.

Dawson City

At the junction of State Highway 2 and the Taylor Highway, I said goodbye to Chicken. I then took a left towards Whitehorse.

After 16 hours we reached Dawson with the guy driving. He made a bee-line for the gambling casino, Diamond Tooth Gertie's.

After a few hours, we headed for his apartment complex. He owned several rental units and he had one vacant that he said I could use free of charge for the duration of my stay. I took him up on the offer and stayed in Dawson for a week.

Many sights in Dawson commemorate the Gold Rush days and celebrate the writers who recorded the phenomenon of the gold rush. Jack London, author of *White Fang*, and, *Call of The Wild*, most notably, recorded the privations suffered by the prospectors in the Klondike. London suffered malnourishment and resultant scurvy himself as a 22 year-old prospector in the gold fields.

Robert Service, called, The Bard Of The Yukon, for his work, *The Shooting Of Dan McGrew*, and Pierre Berton, a local author of 50 books, whose father had been in on the 1898 Klondike Gold Rush, are also honored in Dawson.

I spent my time touring the Yukon River, the widest river I have ever seen except for the Amazon. I took the ferry across and toured through the woods into a field of poisonous muscaria mushrooms. On another hike I went over to the confluence of the Klondike and Yukon Rivers.

Dawson is an interesting town with boardwalks along the streets and lots of tourist shops in 1880s storefronts. Outside of town the landscape looks like a strip mine. The dredges had piled up tailings, the piles of stones and gravel that is left after sluicing out the gold.

The Dawson City Visitor's Center was an interesting visit with much gold rush memorabilia and information about the work of the dredges.

These multi story wood structures worked in the streams and in alluvial soils of rivers and streambeds to scoop up gravel and separate stones through a series of rotating drums with varying size holes. The dredge dropped the large boulders and stones behind the machine early in the process. The gold was contained in the finer sand deposits which were run through a series of inclined sluices with water running over them. The gold being the heaviest element settled out of the sand and dropped to the bottom where a series of small barricades caught it. Eventually most of the sand and mud was washed away to leave the heavier gold.

Home

After a week I was ready to leave Dawson but found an interesting wrinkle in the protocol for leaving the town. I could not take a van from Dawson because I had not entered by a Canada-based van. I could only book travel by air. The van operators were as puzzled as I was about this rule but I complied and, instead of going to another city in Canada, I booked a flight to Seattle.

I arrived in Freemont and visited my friends again. I stayed until the end of August.

I wanted to be back in Missouri in early September to harvest my crop of garlic. I looked forward to many good salads with garlic dressing through the Fall and early Winter.

"Travel does not exist without home....If we never return to the place we started, we would just be wandering, lost. Home is a reflecting surface, a place to measure our growth and enrich us after being infused with the outside world."
Josh Gates,
"Destination Truth: Memoirs of a Monster Hunter."

Travel

January came and so did boredom with the Missouri weather. I dislike with the same intensity hot dry weather and cold windy weather. My house in Springfield offers both.

I could blame it on the house or blame Missouri for that matter but this story started as a confession and will end the same way; I will own up to the truth, I love to travel.

I finished the travel book I was reading and prepared to closed up the house. The following morning I booked a long bus ride.

As the bus rolled through Missouri in a southerly direction I sat back to savor the great memories of trips to the Antarctic and Arctic Oceans. I was traveling again but this time I would not go to the extremes of the earth's cold at 90 degrees latitude. I would instead head towards the Equator and stop at latitude 15. I needed some time in one place and that place would be a warm beach. I was headed for the Pacific Coast at Oaxaca Mexico and a few winter months on the beach at Zipolite.

187

"because he had no place he could stay in without getting tired of it and because there was nowhere to go but everywhere, keep rolling under the stars..."

Jack Kerouac, On the Road